THE MATHEMATICS OF
DIVORCE AND REMARRIAGE

Copyright © 2018 by Gregory A.R. Watt @ Copyright Registration Services

All rights reserved. This book or any portion thereof may not be reproduced or used in any manner whatsoever without the express written permission of the publisher except for the use of brief quotations in a book review.

Printed in the United States of America

First Printing, 2018
Second Printing, 2019
Third Printing 2021

ISBN 978-0-578-89692-2

Cover design: Custom Photo House
Book Formatting: Marvelous Love Ministries

Marvelous Love Ministries:
e-mail: marvelousloveministries@gmail.com

Published by

THE MATHEMATICS OF DIVORCE AND RE-MARRIAGE

(GOD HATES DIVORCE!)

TABLE OF CONTENTS

1. Foreword.. 4

2. **Chapter One**: *GOD HATES DIVORCE!*... 10

   Sub-Titles:

   - Until Death Do Us Part
   - Divorced And Re-Married – What??!!
   - God Hates Divorce! What Does This Scripture Mean?
   - Why Does God Hate Divorce?

3. **Chapter Two:** WHAT GOD HAS PUT TOGETHER, LET NO MAN PUT ASUNDER

   Sub-Titles:

   - What Makes A Man And A Woman Become One Flesh?
   - Why The Marriage Ceremony Then?
   - What God Has Joined Together, Let Not Man Put Asunder!
   - For Better Or Worse!

4. **Chapter Three:** THE COVENANT BREAKER!.. 20

   Sub-Titles:

   - How Is The Covenant Broken?
   - What Is The Other Covenant Breaker?
   - The Exception Clause!

5. **Chapter Four:** CAN CHRISTIANS DIVORCE FOR ANY REASON?...................... 24

   Sub-Titles:
   - Divorced For Any Reason – Am I Still Saved!
   - Adulterer For The Rest Of Your Life?
   - Sex After Divorce.

6. **Chapter Five:** IF DIVORCED ARE YOU CONDEMNED TO LIVE SINGLE.............9

7. **Chapter Six:** WHAT IF YOU ARE DIVORCED MULTIPLE TIMES?......................35

   Sub-Titles:
   - Everyone Is Guilty Of Being A Divorcee!
   - Divorcee? Back Bench!

8. **Chapter Seven:** WHAT DOES "THE HARDNESS OF YOUR HEART" MEAN?.......41

   Sub-Title:
   - The Woman Caught In The Act Of Adultery!

9. **Chapter Eight:** DIVORCED AND REMARRIED BUT STILL NOT FREE!...............46

   Sub-Titles:
   - The Back-Sliders
   - The Saved, But Single
   - The Married, But Not Married
   - Divorced And Remarried - Yikes!

10. **Chapter Nine:** THIS DIVORCE MADNESS MUST STOP!....................... 50

    Sub-Title:
    - Turn Pre And Post-Marital Counselling Into Full Time Ministries

Sub-Sub-Titles:

    I.   What Will On-Going Pre-Marital Counselling Achieve?

    II.   What Will On-Going Post-Marital Counselling Achieve?

- How To Deal With Wrongful Submission Expectations.
- When The Wife Becomes Submissive, What Happens Next?
- Be Mindful Of Whose Covering You Go Under In Marriage.
- Build Your Relationship With Good Foundation.

11. <u>Chapter 10</u>: A MARRIAGE SANCTIONED BY GOD CAN DIE!..............................60

Sub-Title:

- Unfaithfulness - The Notorious Killer!
- Put On The Bond Of Perfection!

CONCLUSION:..67

Grace Makes Provision For Restoration

ADDITIONAL READ AT THE BACK:

An exciting short story of four young Christian girls who found love, but who had their struggles as it relates to their approach to dating and courtship, balanced on the merit of their faith in Jesus Christ and their Church's doctrine.

THE PANGS OF PURITY!

FOREWORD

I grew up in the Pentecostal church. I was taught from the Bible (and rightly so) that God hates divorce. With that, I grew up believing that if Christians marry and wind up becoming divorcees, those persons' lives are over as it relates to remarrying because both parties are still alive. I also believed that if one of the parties committed adultery, then the perpetrator cannot enact a divorce and cannot remarry, but the victim can do both. That would leave the one who committed the act woefully single for the rest of his or her life.

I will not state that that is precisely what had been taught to me growing up, but somehow that is the conviction that I held.

I subsequently got married in 1990 at the age of 24.

I had joined the Jamaica Defense Force two years prior, in 1988. I served for six years as a Rifleman and as an Office Clerk. When I enlisted, I was a devout Christian but then a short while after marriage, maybe about a year or so later, I allowed peer pressure to steer me away from the straight and narrow. I tasted infidelity and just couldn't stop afterwards.

My now way-ward, womanizing lifestyle, as would be expected, began to take its ugly toll on my marriage. The relationship became rocky. Nonetheless, we stayed together for about 13 years until I moved out to live with a woman around 2003. My wife and I stayed separated until about 2011 (approximately eight years) when I filed for divorce. MY GOD! The unthinkable had happened to me! I was getting a divorce!

After a divine intervention, I had returned to the Lord in 2010. The Lord had been dealing with me before then, but what kept me from re-committing my life fully to the Lord was the fact that I was now in a dilemma – according to what I grew up believing about divorce and remarriage I knew that I was in trouble. The belief I held dictated that my wife could file for divorce because I had been the unfaithful one. But knowing her, she would not do that.

I tried "lighting a candle, singing a Sankey," and tried reconciling with her. We went to counselling but to no avail. She wanted nothing to do with me, but she (holding the same belief about divorce and remarriage as I did) refused to divorce me. I think part of me was holding onto a slim hope that if she did the divorce, perhaps there was a way that I could "squeeze" a remarriage and maybe, just maybe God would not be too vexed.

Reality hit me that God will not water down His principles to accommodate anyone. A feeling of hopelessness began to engulf me. There seemed to be no way out for me. I couldn't get my marriage back (couldn't blame her though) and she, being the victim, wasn't about to exercise her rights to divorce me. I began to feel what the prophet Isaiah must have felt when he said: "Woe is me, for I am undone…!" I was between a rock and a hard place!

One day, in desperation, I just fell to my knees and began to talk to GOD. I cried: 'Lord, I fear Your name. I do not want to be guilty of adding or taking away from Your words. You see my situation. It's hopeless for me. But suddenly, after all these years of blindly holding onto a belief system, I now realise that something doesn't seem so right with this doctrine that I hold. Lord, the reality is that I cannot see how it would be possible for me to live single for the rest of my life. Please open up all my understanding wide so that I can fully know this whole thing about divorce and remarriage.' And He did! Glory to God! I soon learned by the revelation knowledge of God that **"GRACE is never fully understood or appreciated until one reaches that point in one's life where GRACE is fully needed."**

I was not desiring to water down the gospel. It was about understanding the gospel. **St. James 1:5** says that *'if anyone lacks wisdom he should ask of God and He will honour the request and will not deny revelation of the truth.'*

A DIVINE VISITATION

In 2010 just before I recommitted my life to the Lord, one night I had a vision. My brother, Dalton had died the year before. The Lord sent an Angel to me in the form of my brother, and he asked me when I would give my life back to Jesus Christ.' I said "Dalton when you saw Jesus what did you tell Him about your brothers and sister (I have another brother, Ralston and a sister, Charmaine. I was the eldest)?" In response, he took my hand and flew with me through a window. He took me to what appeared to be the New Testament Church that we all attended (well, that I had also attended until I backslid). I saw Jesus standing outside, but I could not see His face. The Angel took me up into the universe. I saw the word of God popping all over in the constellations like fire-crackers, in rainbow colours. Afterwards, the Angel took me back into the room from where he had taken me. God had anointed me with the knowledge of His words! This fact was confirmed six years to the month when in June 2016 I met a Prophet R.A. Mckenzie from Jamaica for the first time. He called me out from the congregation and began to prophesy to me. He told me about that angelic visitation and how God anointed me with the knowledge of

His word. To God be the glory! He always confirms His words. After my divine encounter in 2010, I began to understand the word of God as I never comprehended it before. I would now like to share the revelation of this very present and poignant issue regarding divorce and remarriage that plagues us. Read on, but please note: This is no new doctrine or new revelation. **Deuteronomy 29:29** says:

"The secret things belong unto the LORD our God: but those things which are revealed belong unto us and to our children forever, that we may do all the words of this law."

Moreover: *"For other foundation can no man lay than that is laid, which is Jesus Christ." - 1 Corinthians 3:11.*

And: *"...though we, or an angel from heaven, preach any other gospel unto you than that which we have preached unto you, let him be accursed." - Galatians 1:8.*

This truth has always been with us. It's just that many persons merely gloss over the written word and run away with their own interpretation and have taught men their doctrine.

We grapple with many points of doctrine because we do not spend quality time with the Lord and allow His Blessed Holy Spirit, the Spirit of truth to lead us into all truth. Also because some of us, even though we approach God for the fact, do not genuinely empty ourselves of personal ideals to hear the heart of God. **St. James 3: 1 & 2** states that *'we must not be many teachers because we offend in many things.'* Hence we have so many whom, though they call on the name of the Lord Jesus, wind up creating different denominations. Are there divisions in Christ? Absolutely not! Therefore, where there is a denomination, there is a division. Where there is a division, there is a deficit. A deficit is a fault. Therefore, God would not expect us to trust our souls to an entity that is faulty. He instructs us to put all our belief into that one Person Who is perfect, which is Jesus Christ, His Son! It is therefore of great importance that we do not blindly accept everything that we are taught, simply because our pastor is teaching it. We all have a responsibility and a right through Jesus Christ to have a personal relationship with God, just like the Berean Jews in **Acts 17:11** who embraced that right.

At the mount of transfiguration (documented in **St. Matthew 17 and St. Luke 9**) we see where Peter, being so overwhelmed by the awesomeness of the revelation, wanted to create three different denominations right there - worship for Jesus, Moses and Elijah. God the Father had to straighten him out immediately. So I am never hung up on what denomination to attend. As long as they preach Jesus and Him crucified and not their church doctrine, I am good. It is God's divine will that *' we* *should all come into the full knowledge of His revealed truth* **(1 Timothy 2:4).'**

In **St. Matthew 24:15** Jesus was teaching about the unfolding of prophetic fulfillments regarding world events. He never said that they should wait for new divine revelations from Heaven to understand when these prophecies were being fulfilled. He said:

*"**When ye, therefore shall see the abomination of desolation, spoken of by Daniel the prophet, stand in the holy place, (whoso readeth, let him understand:)**"*

The three wise men who found Jesus when He was born did not get any new revelation to know when Christ would be born. They diligently studied what God had already revealed in written form and followed the signs.

What I am about to write is not an anomaly that can place me on a pedestal that says, out of the generations of men God has risen one who knows what none of us has ever understood. God never leaves His words lacking for witnesses in any age, and the scriptures are not given by secret interpretation **(2 Peter 1:20)**. Even David, who lived during the dispensation of Law, understood the concept of Grace, even before it was revealed through Jesus Christ. He was able to comprehend and embrace the knowledge of the workings of Grace because he was never satisfied with mere, ritualistic worship. David went for the jugular - the heart of God, where full understanding lies. Hence God said that *'David was a man who went after His very heart.'* - **(1 Samuel 13:14 and Acts 13:22)**.

Abraham was another man whom I greatly admire. Even before the law itself was handed down, Abraham understood the workings of Grace. He knew that the only way to be right with God was to piggy-back on God's righteousness. He authenticated his faith with his actions, just like we are told to do in **St. James 1:17**. He thus became righteous, and God called him His friend **(St. James 2:23)**.

Over the centuries, there have been many who have come to this truth of which I am about to write. There are theological scholars, Bishops and Pastors of our time who already have the full knowledge concerning this issue, but I have never seen any teaching on the subject that I can speak about. I am not saying that there isn't any. I am just saying that I am not privy to it. At least not in any of the churches that I had ever attended.

Maybe the religious leaders are afraid to release the truth, for fear that the divorce rate might get out of control. But it already has. Hiding the truth will not solve the problem. And the issue regarding wrongful belief about remarriage will only intensify and keep us in bondage, because of ignorance. I believe that, instead of people embarking on a mad rush to get a divorce, following the release of the information, proper, in-depth and balanced teaching, on the other hand, would stem the flow rather than intensify it.

Recruit Training 1988 - Newcastle, Jamaica (at age 22)

NO. 2 SQUAD

SQUAD CORPORAL

CPL. McCALLA N.

JDF/23751 PTE WATT, G
VALE ROYAL (JAMAICA) - 1990

Seated L - R: Recs. DaCosta D. Cousley

Standing L - R: Recs. Watt G. Robinson I

Chapter 1:

GOD HATES DIVORCE!

I will dedicate the first chapter to point out the fact that this book is not about campaigning for people to go out and get a divorce. And it's not about God endorsing separation. It's about God wanting us to have proper knowledge of His divine will and His doctrine in every aspect.

In **1 Corinthians 7** after dealing with a flurry of marital issues, Paul closed verse 15 by stating that '***God has called us to peace.***' When bombarded by all the complexities of marriage and the various things that can cause a break-up, and when the dust is settled, unless we know the heart of God on the end of the matter, we will be in torments and bondages, not knowing where we stand. God gets no glory when we stand in ignorance. In **Hosea 4:6** God noted that ***'His people were destroyed from lack of knowledge.'*** **St. James 1:5** says that ***'any man who lacks knowledge should ask God for it and that God will not hold back the knowledge but will give it freely.'***

To preach a particular word, though it might be very nice to hear, if it's not the word of God, in the real essence of His intended meaning, it will not profit the hearer. And vice versa, if it's a message of doom, but God never sent it, it's useless. Hence, Paul the Apostle said that ***'if we preach that Christ was raised from the dead'*** and it's not right (though the thought is very lovely that Christ is raised and we would follow), it will not profit us who believe, and our faith would be in vain **(1 Corinthians. 15)**. But thanks be to God that this message is real! Glory to God! Hallelujah!

Similarly if one teaches that it's OK or that it's wrong to get a divorce and remarry, the most important thing is not what one believes but what the facts, according to God's words, and it's chore meanings say. That is what will please God and what will profit us. If God didn't say it, it's not it. If it's not God's meaning, it's meaningless.

In **Malachi 2:16** Jehovah God makes it quite clear that He hates divorce. This verse has been resonating within the Church for centuries. The blind adherence to this passage of scripture has caused many a marriage, that could have and maybe should have ended in divorce, to stay together. But is this good? Not necessarily.

Until Death Do Us Part

While there are those who boast a lot of calendar years of marriage, truth be told many of those marriages had died and had been buried for most of those many years, but because they hold fast to the doctrine that God hates divorce they relegate themselves to suffering in silence and putting up appearances. Something inside their minds has convinced them that they just have to bear that suffering until death parted them and that staying in that facade of marriage, despite it being dead, would pay homage to God and that He would be pleased. But the opposite is true. Appearances do not glorify God. Favourable results do. If we do not benefit in our marriage, as with anything else, God gets no glory! The glory of God emanates from our benefit.

I am indeed not inferring that a dead marriage cannot come back to life, but it's up to the parties involved to decide whether or not the marriage comes back into fruitfulness. As a matter of truth, God would heartily rejoice at restoration as opposed to a divorce. The whole mission of God the Father, His Son Jesus Christ and the Blessed Holy Spirit are to heal and restore humanity back to every good thing that they had lost. So there are two options: repair your marriage or get the hell out! If its dead, not stressing you out and you are both OK with the arrangement, for whatever reason, and you can stay right there, then there is no law against that. But if the marriage remains dead, has decayed and is buried and has no hope of coming back to life, and it's sucking the life out of you, there will be no additional star in your crown for bearing it through to your death. It could be the death of you – spiritually and physically. Get the hell out of it! But restore if it is possible.

Divorce must be the very last option when all else fails. Need I say that Jesus never fails? But God will only do what we allow Him to do. He will not violate our right to choose.

If you do get divorced, however, this does not mean that you have to remarry. But what if you do? Will God send you to hell for it? We'll see.

Divorce And Remarried – What??!!

The other outlook on the fact that God hates divorce is that if one does get a divorce and have remarried, then that couple is for the rest of their lives living an adulterous lifestyle. This view is an error in the doctrine of Jesus Christ that has caused many to be ostracized by the church, their family and their friends. Because, they say, God hates divorce! Jesus says in **St. John 16:2** that *'there are those who will put you out of the Church…thinking that they are doing the will of God.'* Those divorcee-haters who put you at the back of the church and who prevent you from doing service in church are right down the alley for this scripture to be fulfilled against them.

God Hates Divorce! What does this scripture mean?

By their actions, whole churches have taken this scripture to mean that if one gets divorced and subsequently remarries, as long as they live together as man and wife they are living in sin, because the divorced spouse is still alive. Thus their souls are in danger of burning in hell.

This view could not be further from the truth, and that mode of belief is adding to the scriptures because of an error in understanding. There is no hidden or deep meaning here. The scripture says that God "hates" divorce. That is not the same thing as saying if you happen to get a divorce I won't forgive you. It simply means just what it says: God "hates" it.

Why Does God Hate Divorce?

Our Heavenly Father is a God of love. In His presence is the fullness of joy and at His right hand are pleasures forever. What makes Heaven such an excellent place to live is the harmony that prevails there. Divorce brings disharmony. In its wake, it brings heart-breaks; regrets; great pains for the divorcees; the children; the

Church; the community and everything else that comes with a broken home. The status of the home bears the chore fabric for the stability of our church, community, nation and the world. If family values are diminished, and if there are more broken homes than stable ones, it's like a domino effect, everything else gets affected. God hates that. However, because we are faulty people in a fallen world, God knows that though He hates divorce, it will happen. The Lord does not and will never endorse separation. But if it happens, He will not condemn us for divorcing, and He will not condemn us for remarrying. Grace is there to fill every need.

We now understand that I am not promoting divorce and that I am not in any way saying that God encourages separation. I will endeavour, according to the knowledge that was opened up to me, to explain that while scripture does not endorse it, if divorce and remarriage happen you are not condemned to hell, and why.

CHAPTER 2:

WHAT GOD HAS JOINED TOGETHER, LET NO MAN PUT ASUNDER!

*A*fter receiving his wife, Adam, being perfect, and filled with the Spirit of wisdom from God, prophesied and said:

"…This is now bone of my bones, and flesh of my flesh: she shall be called Woman, because she was taken out of Man.

[24] Therefore shall a man leave his father and his mother, and shall cleave unto his wife: and they shall be one flesh" (Genesis 2: 23 & 24).

The Lord Jesus endorsed this word by saying, *"What God has joined together, let no man put asunder (St. Matthew 19:6 and St. Mark 10:9* speak to this).

For us to understand why man (referring to a Judge) has no power to render a marriage null and void, first we must understand what makes a man and woman become one flesh in the first place.

What Makes A Man And A Woman Become One Flesh?

SEX and not the marriage ceremony is what makes a man and a woman become one flesh! The marriage Rites give the couple the legal rights before God and man to become one flesh. The sexual act affirms the bond in the spiritual realm, and it is then that the couple becomes truly united. On the other hand, because the sexual act is the divine rule that creates the bond, a man and woman can become one flesh without getting married first. Why? Simple. The law that God had set for one-ness of flesh is not determined by whether or not a marriage ceremony has occurred. Sexual intercourse is what makes that bond. However, in such a case where sexual intercourse happens without the couple first getting married, it would be an illegal one-ness before God. He calls it fornication. But if they get married first, then engage in the sexual act, He said: *"marriage is honourable... and the bed undefiled.. (Hebrews 12:4)."* For God to give accent, the natural and the spiritual must come into agreement in that order, and there cannot be one without the other, as it is with all things in every sphere of creation. The natural must hold hands with the spiritual for there to be a manifestation.

For one to understand the principles for one-ness of flesh that God has to honour, whether, the couple is legally married or not (note, I did not say that God accepts a fornicating lifestyle. I am pointing out that He sets rules and He honours those principles), here is an excellent example of a law being honoured despite the manner in which it was carried out: according to the divine rule that God has set forth for a woman to conceive (which is sexual intercourse between herself and a man), whether the sex was consensual or she was raped; whether she was married or not; as long as the sperm is able; and she is naturally able to conceive; she could still become impregnated, even though she was raped and is not married to the man.

Here is another one – the thieves on the Cross. One was lost, not because Jesus did not want to save him, but because he followed the principle that God had set forth for death – rejection of the Saviour! The other thief, however, received his ticket to Paradise because he accepted the principle that God had set forth for his salvation, which was to receive Jesus as Lord and Saviour. God and Jesus could not and would not have rejected him then because he followed the laid down principles that guaranteed him entrance into Heaven.

God does not guide His decisions by frivolous feelings and emotions like that of human passions. He operates by the rules, regulations and principles that He had decreed. And they were all enacted for our benefits and not out of selfish motives as we humans usually do. **Hebrews 12: 9 & 10** says *"Furthermore we have had fathers of our flesh which corrected us, and we gave them reverence: shall we not much rather be in subjection unto the Father of spirits, and live? For they verily for a few days chastened us after their own pleasure; but he for our profit, that we might be partakers of his holiness."*

Now please don't be confused here because this scripture speaks about chastisement. The lesson to glean in this moment is that God operates at a higher and more righteous level of purpose, with clear, precise motives, for our benefit and not selfishly or out of fleeting emotions.

How do I know that sexual intercourse is what makes the bond and not the marriage ceremony? Read **1 Corinthians 6:16**. It warns: *"What? Know ye not that he which is joined to an harlot is one body? For two, saith he, shall be one flesh."* Persons who go into harlots do not marry them. They simply go in and have sex with them. After that sexual encounter, despite the fact that both persons had just committed a sinful act, God still has to recognize the rule that He had set for **one-ness** of the flesh, which is not the marriage ceremony but the sexual act, because He is a God of order, and He honours His words. It is just that in such a case God is not pleased with that one-ness because it is illegal. And the broader meaning here for harlot is that 'a man must not have sex with a woman who is not his wife, because we sin against God by creating an illegal one-ness of flesh, which is called fornication.'

Why The Marriage Ceremony Then?

If sex, and not the marriage ceremony is what makes a man and woman become one flesh, why does one need to get married?

For further comprehension, this truth must be understood: everything in scripture has its greater meaning spiritually. There are two laws at work here. It is the natural and the spiritual. The physical is a shadow or an example of the supernatural things. Therefore it is of lesser value and must never be seen as first law. If two virgins marry but never consummate the relationship, there is no agreement in the divine realm. They can claim to be legally married, but they cannot say that they are one flesh. Marriage ceremony in the natural imitates the marriage ceremony in the supernatural realm, and this divine grant of one-ness becomes effective when sexual intercourse happens between the two after the marriage ceremony.

In Abrahamic times, there was no marital law. God did not, at that time hand down the Ten Commandments. Therefore, Abraham lived even before the dispensation of law. Thus there was no tabled marital law. The law of conscience was in operation then. If a man saw a woman whom he wished to become his wife, once he is successful in wooing her, he would just take her to his tent and sleep with her. As soon as they have sex, she became his wife, simply because the sexual act made them become one flesh. In God's sight the same principles for faithfulness would apply, and thus God honoured the union on that basis. And equally, just as there was no written marital law, there was also no divorce law. But rules are created when atrocities are committed.

"Every good gift and every perfect gift is from above, and cometh down from the Father of lights, with whom is no variableness, neither shadow of turning." So says **St. James 1:17**, but because we are imperfect human beings, living in a fallen world, usually after the good things of God reaches our hands, we corrupt it.

God never uttered "thou shalt not kill" until men began to commit murders. Likewise, because some men would make wives through intercourse but then after having tasted the goods, reneged on their commitment, it became necessary to enact a marital law to protect the displaced party. Equally, a divorce was merely a verbal occurrence. But then, because in Moses' law if a married woman was found guilty of having sexual intercourse with another man she was stoned to death, and just as how many would lie about having slept with the woman, thus making her his wife, equally many would also lie that they had verbally divorced the woman. Therefore, I am confident that many innocent women were stoned to death after having been seen with another man, in the wake of a verbal divorce. To prevent this wickedness, just as how a marriage law was created, Moses had to develop a divorce law to stop these atrocities from being committed against innocent women. Moses was never endorsing divorce, as Jesus had pointed out. He was merely forced to create a law to stem the flow of this wickedness.

So now that a marriage law was created, the old law of conscience was abolished. It thus became illegal to just sleep with a woman and call her your wife. The spiritual principle of what constitutes the one-ness of flesh still held but, without adherence to the newly enacted marital laws, God would now view such an act as fornication.

But, if sexual intercourse, and not the marriage ceremony is what makes the man and woman become one flesh, why still do I need to get married?

Romans 13:1 of the English Standard Version (ESV) Bible declares: *"Let every* *person be subject to the governing authorities. For there is no authority except from God, and those that exist have been instituted by God."* So once there is an enacted law within the land we are commanded to obey the laws of the land, as long as they do not contradict the higher commandments of God. Therefore, the marriage ceremony makes it legal before God and man for the two persons to become joined together as one flesh, but it is the act of consummation that creates the spiritual bond and seals the deal.

What God Has Joined Together, Let Not Man Put Asunder!

It simply means then, that what God has sealed by His spiritual principles - that which makes the covenant between the man and the woman, which is sexual intercourse, a Judge's seal and signature have no power to break. Therefore, if the covenant is not broken, though a Judge may sign and seal the divorce decree, in the spiritual realm, the two persons are still considered bonded before God!

Wow! My God! What is this?

Let's go to chapter 3, but before we do I must deal very quickly and succinctly with the marital oath that was inspired by this word of God which says: "what God has joined together, let not man put asunder." It is the vow: "For better or worse!"

For Better Or Worse!

"The Pharisees also came unto him, tempting him, and saying unto him, Is it lawful for a man to put away his wife for every cause?

⁴ And he answered and said unto them, Have ye not read, that he which made them at the beginning made them male and female,

⁵ And said, For this cause shall a man leave father and mother, and shall cleave to his wife: and they twain shall be one flesh?

⁶ Wherefore they are no more twain, but one flesh. What therefore God hath joined together, let not man put asunder." – St. Matthew 19: 3 - 6

Jesus very clearly is saying that ' marriage is a ride-or-die event – through thick or thin!' Hence, at the marriage ceremony, we accede to the oath "for better or worse, until death do us part."

I just told you that every good and perfect gift comes from God, but once it reaches the hand of man we usually corrupt that good thing. Many a husband and wife have used this beautiful oath which was inspired by the word of God as a manipulative tool to keep their partner subdued in a degrading, pointless and sometimes even dangerous relationship. They have no desire to change but want their partner to 'accept them for who they are.' This term does not mean: take me with my bad habits. It means accept me for the way God made me and whom God made me to be.

Scenario – a man beats his wife incessantly then when she wants to leave him he would say, "honey, remember that we were married for better or worse." Then the poor woman would once more subject herself to the union while trembling in fear for her life.

"For better or worse…" means we stick together through the natural happenstance of life. "For better or worse…" does not come under deliberate projectiles that we fire into our relationship, then expect our spouse to stay subjected to that. That is manipulation - witchcraft - obeah!

CHAPTER 3: THE COVENANT BREAKER!

HOW IS THE COVENANT BROKEN?

eath!

"The wife is bound by the law as long as her husband liveth; but if her husband be dead, she is at liberty to be married to whom she will; only in the Lord." – 1 Corinthians 7:39

So then, by this scripture, the covenant can only be broken by death! But why death?

It is quite simple. While the two persons are alive they both will continue to enjoy intimacy together. If and when death occurs, that would not be possible anymore. It would then be impractical for God to hold the surviving spouse (whether it's the woman or man) to the covenant. Thus he or she is free to remarry whomever they will, but to a fellow Christian, as Paul is saying here because the chapter was addressing Christians regarding marriage.

This point is clear. Therefore, it is not necessary to belabour the point any further. However, even though this scripture seems to be saying that only death can break the oath, this is not the case. The covenant can also be severed another way. And while both persons are alive. Let's go there!

WHAT IS THE OTHER COVENANT BREAKER?

Infidelity!

If one or both persons cheat on each other, that breaks the covenant of one-ness of flesh! Let me prove it.

In **St. Matthew 5:31 & 32** Jesus taught *"It hath been said, Whosoever shall put away his wife, let him give her a writing of divorcement: But I say unto you, That whosoever shall put away his wife, saving for the cause of fornication, causeth her to commit adultery: and whosoever shall marry her that is divorced commit- teth adultery."*

It is quite interesting that Jesus opened this topic by saying. "it hath been said…" Who was the person who had said it? Moses, the approved servant of the Lord, had said it and now Jesus seems to be refuting Moses! It was Moses indeed who had enacted the divorce law in Israel. In the previous chapter I pointed out that verbal divorce was so frivolous and un-binding it left the divorced person at a disadvantage because, unless the divorcer confirms that he had divorced his wife, she had no way of proving that he had done so. Therefore, to prevent this from happening, Moses decreed that for a divorce to be recognized as such the divorcer must present a Bill of divorcement. That way he cannot conveniently deny it, and she would have had her proof. Did poor ol'Moses do something wrong? Certainly not. To better understand why Jesus seemed to be putting aside Moses' decree let's go once again to **St. Matthew chapter 19**.

I would imagine that even before Moses had outlawed verbal divorcement and commanded that only a formal written Decree would be honoured, the men were divorcing their wives for almost every reason. But undoubtedly the divorce rate was not stemmed by the new law. Perhaps if anything, it got worse. The power of the written proof probably emboldened them to divorce with even more frequency.

During His ministry, Jesus made His take on divorce quite clear. Hence, now at verse 3 of the chapter, The Pharisees came to pit Him against Moses. They thought that they could catch Him in a trap and thus turn the people against Him because Moses was revered as a great Prophet amongst the people. One just does not disrespect Moses in Israel. They asked, tempting Him: *"…Is it lawful for a man to put away his wife for every cause?"* Jesus' response reiterated the fact that when the man and woman become one flesh by the laid down divine principles, not even Moses' divorce law could break that covenant. And this is what is essential to observe – **what makes and breaks the bond!** So then, while it is true that death breaks the union, said covenant could also be severed by one other way while both parties are alive – Infidelity!

Yes, Infidelity – fornication or adultery – sexual sin! How is this so? Simple: the same thing that makes the covenant can break it. Ever hear the saying, only a Ninja can kill a Ninja? If sex is what makes the bond then naturally if either of the two persons has sex with someone else they break the covenant. That is why in verse 9 Jesus said: *"And I say unto you, Whosoever shall put away his wife, except it be for fornication, and shall marry another, committeth adultery: and whoso marrieth her which is put away doth commit adultery."* So where-in we had seen before and during Moses' divorce law where men were divorcing their wives for any reason, here we see Jesus proffering an exception clause for divorce and remarriage. Of course, the Pharisees wanted to place blame on Moses, practically stating that 'Moses had legalized divorce.' But Jesus explained that though Moses created the law, it was not because he endorsed it, but he had to bring law and order to the unfortunate ordeal and that it was they, on the other hand, who, by their unforgiving hearts were making divorce such a lucrative venture.

The Exception Clause!

"EXCEPT it be for fornication…" This is called the exception clause for divorce. As I said before, wherein, before Jesus came, they were prone to divorce for every cause or reason, Jesus here is saying that 'the only divorce and remarriage that would not attract the charge of adultery was if infidelity had occurred.' But why the exception to the rule though?

After Jesus sharply out-lawed divorce for every cause in **St. Matthew 19: 4 to 6**, here in verse 9 He declares an exception to the rule. Did Jesus do this just because He was sympathetic to the person's pain of being cheated on and so was announcing a free pass for the victim to divorce the perpetrator? No! A resounding NO!

I had said earlier that God operates by divine rules, regulations and principles. If I accept Jesus Christ as Lord and Saviour and serve Him to the end God and Jesus would have no choice but to take me into Heaven because I would be in line with the divine principles, that which makes it legal for me to enter Heaven's gates. Likewise, when Jesus gave the exception clause, it was on the basis of what made the covenant in the first place. Sexual intercourse! Therefore, by the same token, since the man and woman became one flesh through consummation, if either of the party has sex with someone else the first covenant is broken, and the perpetrator has now effectively established a new bond or one-ness of flesh with the person with whom he or she had committed adultery.

In all of this, Jesus was still not endorsing divorce. He was merely pointing out that if they were inclined to get divorced, a divorce for any other reason, other than infidelity (though it was legal in the natural realm according to Moses' law), a remarriage would be spiritually illegal. The reason why remarriage in this respect would be considered unlawful is that divorce for every other reason apart from infidelity would mean that the covenant was still intact. While both parties are alive nothing else could break the agreement but sexual intercourse, the same thing that made the agreement in the first place.

In theological circles, there have been debates about Jesus' usage of the words fornication and Adultery in the passage of scripture. There is a correlation between fornication and adultery. They both speak of the same thing – a sexual sin! Therefore, I would not get hung up on that. Once the sexual act is committed, the covenant is broken. No one must take this as a license to go and get a divorce though. **GOD HATES DIVORCE! GOD LOVES RECONCILIATION!** Therefore, if the two persons, even after adultery is committed, can both forgive the act and move forward in a renewed relationship with each other, Heaven will applaud that. But if they decide to go their separate ways, in that case, because the covenant has already been severed, both parties can remarry, and it doesn't matter at that point who broke the covenant. It's broken! And God is prepared to restore both parties and recognize them in a new union.

***Further to the exception clause, Jesus was speaking more so about the spiritual divorce and remarriage as opposed to just the natural or legal divorce and remarriage, because, if someone divorces for other reasons other than infidelity, remarries, but never ever consummates the new marriage, the charge of adultery could never be applied, though the person had remarried. Adultery can only be committed through sexual intercourse. Flip-side, if the person never legally remarries, but has a sexual relationship with someone else, then that person would have spiritually divorced and remarried, even if it was not legally (naturally).

But what if a divorce does happen for any other reason other than infidelity. What happens then? Does it mean that both parties have to stay unmarried for the remainder of their natural lives or if they remarry will they be considered adulterers for the rest of their lives? Mm!

Let's go to the next chapter.

***Added after first publication.

CHAPTER 4: CAN CHRISTIANS DIVORCE FOR ANY REASON?

*Y*es! The answer is yes!

Christians can divorce for any reason that the law of the land will allow. For example, desertion, abuse (physical and mental), defamation of character (bringing the other Party into disrepute), etc. Anyone of these is horrible for a spouse or both persons to have to endure. Therefore, if a Christian is experiencing this kind of dilemma that person can indeed file for divorce. Of course, divorce must always be the very last option. If the matter can be adequately resolved through counselling, prayer and whatever other suitable means which brings about beneficial, sustainable change, then kudos to that couple. However, if a mend cannot be achieved and the relationship breaks down irretrievably, then divorce might be the option to take.

Nonetheless, despite the horrible trauma that any such issue might cause one or both Parties, Jesus, allowing Himself to be guided by divine principles, judged that 'if a divorce and remarriage occurs for any other reason other than infidelity, then the one causes the other to commit adultery (in the event of that person getting intimate with someone else because of the separation). The divorcer also commits adultery if he or she remarries and the new spouse is also guilty of sin having slept with the divorcer.' So says the Lord right here in **St. Matthew 19:9:**

"And I say unto you, Whosoever shall put away his wife, except it be for fornication, and shall marry another, committeth adultery: and whoso marrieth her which is put away doth commit adultery."

Here it is re-iterated again in **Romans 7: 2 & 3:**

"2. For the woman which hath an husband is bound by the law to her husband so long as he liveth; but if the husband be dead, she is loosed from the law of her husband.

3. So then if, while her husband liveth, she be married to another man, she shall be called an adulteress: but if her husband be dead, she is free from that law; so that she is no adulteress, though she be married to another man."

Question: Whoa! This is a heavy hitter! It hits you right in the Solar Plexus! But man, you just said that a Christian could divorce for any reason that the law of the land will allow!

Answer: Yes I did. I just never said anything about remarriage! And the Lord here is speaking about an occurrence of remarriage.

Question: So are you saying that if I divorce or get divorced for any other reason other than adultery, I cannot re-marry?

Answer: I never said that either.

Question: Well then, what are you saying?

Jesus, right here again wasn't speaking according to emotions. The basis of His judgement was on the principles of what constitutes a one-ness of flesh between the man and the woman, which is sexual intercourse. Nothing outside of consummation could make that spiritual bond. In like manner, the only thing that can break that covenant while the parties are alive is one or both persons sleeping with someone else. Any other atrocities outside of sexual intercourse are not powerful enough to break that spiritual bond. Hence Jesus said if one divorces for any other reason other than infidelity and remarries, that person creates a whole sandstorm of adultery from all sides.

Question: So, if I am divorced for any other reason other than infidelity am I still saved. And if I remarry under such terms will I be an adulterer in God's sight for the rest of my life as long as I live in that new marital relationship?

Let's see:

Divorced For Any Reason - Am I Still Saved?

I did say at the beginning of this Chapter that yes, a Christian can divorce for any reason that the law allows. And also, to answer this question: yes if you divorce for any other reason than infidelity you are still saved (now I am not talking about remarriage here. I am dealing with divorce for any other reason than cheating). I can prove it. Let's go to **1 Corinthians 7:10 & 11:**

"And unto the married I command, yet not I, but the Lord, Let not the wife depart from her husband:

[11] But and if she depart, let her remain unmarried or be reconciled to her husband: and let not the husband put away his wife."

Paul here was addressing a situation whereby both parties are Christians, and they get divorced for a reason or reasons other than infidelity. He was speaking on the premise that neither of the two had become intimate with anyone else either before or after the divorce. And he was referring to what Jesus said in **St. Matthew 19:9**.

Though the two are divorced they are still considered saved and thus still a part of the Body of Christ. Thus they would still be in line and entitled to receive continued spiritual guidance.

Once divorced, because it wasn't due to infidelity on either side, they are automatically expected to live celibate because an act of remarriage by either of the two would set off the chain reaction of adultery after the fact. However, if after awhile they realize that they were not cut out to remain single for the rest of their lives, Paul here encourages that the two same persons should reconcile. But why though?

Simple. It doesn't matter how long the two persons are divorced for, as long as neither of them had slept with anyone else before or after their divorce, they are still one flesh in the spiritual realm. Yes! The ink and stamp of the Divorce Judge is not powerful enough to break that spiritual bond, because the Judge's tools are man-made and thus is of lesser authority than that of the spiritual. Just as how the marriage ceremony by itself was not powerful enough to make that bond spiritually, but the sexual act. So if two virgins marry, spend the rest of their lives together as man and wife but never consummate, then they have not become one flesh. By marrying according to the law of the land, they have legal right before God and man to have sex and become one flesh. Hence God said ***"marriage is honourable and the bed undefiled…"*** but if they, being virgins, marry but never consummate then the covenant is not made.

Question: But what if the divorcer or divorcee who is divorced under this category of other reasons other than infidelity cannot contain, and remarry, but to someone else. What then?

Answer: It means that someone just set off the chain reaction of adultery!

Question: So are these persons adulterers for the rest of their lives?

Answer: No! Let's examine this.

Adulterer For The Rest Of Your Life?

St. Matthew 19:9 - *"And I say unto you, Whosoever shall put away his wife, except it be for fornication, and shall marry another, committeth adultery: and whoso marrieth her which is put away doth commit adultery."*

Romans 7: 2 & 3 - *"2. For the woman which hath an husband is bound by the law to her husband so long as he liveth; but if the husband be dead, she is loosed from the law of her* husband.

3. So then if, while her husband liveth, she be married to another man, she shall be called an adulteress: but if her husband be dead, she is free from that law; so that she is no adulteress, though she be married to another man."

So we are right back at these troubling scriptures! But do not despair. There is hope.

Again these scriptures are evidently addressing, not the act of divorcing for any reason. It's dealing with the matter of a remarriage where infidelity was not the cause for divorce. Verse 3 of Romans 7 seems to suggest that if this remarriage occurs then the woman, while her first husband is alive would, for the rest of her life be an adulteress. However, this is not the case.

To better understand this scripture one can look at different biblical translations other than King James Version. Type in the word parallel next to the verse of scripture of your interest in Google, and you will see the different wordings. Personally, I am a bit wary of some of these translations, but after looking at a few parallels of this verse, they all make sense, coupled more so with my now knowledge of what makes and breaks the covenant. Throughout this book, that is the chore of the matter – **what makes and breaks the bond!** It is this factor that determines the spiritual legality of a new covenant and God accepting or rejecting a new marriage. Once that is understood, everything else becomes clear, and therefore we can see that the different translations do not contradict but make sense.

Romans 7:3 King James Version says: *"…if while her husband liveth, she be MARRIED TO ANOTHER MAN, she shall be called an adulteress…"*

Now let's look at a couple parallels to that same verse:

Holman Christian Standard Bible says: *"So then if she GIVES HERSELF TO ANOTHER MAN while her husband is living, she will be called an adulteress…"*

New American Standard Bible says: *"So then if while her husband is living, she is JOINED TO ANOTHER MAN she shall be called an adulteress…"*

Paul in **Romans 7:3** seems to be saying that the woman would be called an adulteress for the rest of her life. But Jesus, here in **St. Matthew 19:9** used the word "doth" or does commit adultery. This word usage seems to suggest a one time charge for the act in the event of a REMARRIAGE. And indeed it is a one-time charge. After which, because they are legally married, God will return and bless the union. To this, let's take a quick look at David and Bathsheba:

After David and Bathsheba had sex, they both became one flesh, so by the time Uriah came home from war, in the spiritual realm, he was not seen as one with his wife anymore. The spiritual realm was now seeing David and Bathsheba as one. But it was an illegal one-ness. Afterwards, they became legally married, and thus they became legally bound, both in the natural and the spiritual.

At this point, the argument can be put forward that death had broken the covenant between Uriah and Bathsheba and that is why God accepted the remarriage. However, observing the principles of what makes and breaks the one-ness of flesh covenant between a man and a woman, we see that yes, while death automatically breaks the covenant, said agreement can also be broken while both spouses are alive, but only by the same thing that made the covenant – sex!

So Uriah never had to die for God to recognize Bathsheba divorcing Uriah and remarrying David. The covenant was already broken through sex. David knew this, but he just wanted to cover up his sin.

Sex After Divorce:

I will proffer two scenarios:

1. Two persons divorce for other reason or reasons other than infidelity. They both engage in sexual intercourse with someone else and do not remarry. As long as they are not legally married, in the initial instance of the act they became adulterers, but afterwards, if they both continue to have intercourse with those new persons, because the covenant is already broken in the spirit realm, with them having established new spiritual agreements with their new partners, their lifestyle now becomes a fornicating one. Fornication because though they are now one-flesh in the spirit through sex, they are not legally married.

2. Two persons divorce for other reason or reasons other than infidelity. Also on the premise that the last person they had sex with was their spouse, they subsequently remarry to other persons. Though divorced, because the reason was not infidelity, in the spirit the covenant is still intact. Hence they are still one flesh. Though **legally divorced.** Now, don't miss this. On the other hand, having now been **lawfully remarried,** each to someone else (let's say they all decide not to have sex until marriage), being now legally married does not automatically make the new couples become one flesh. They cannot become one flesh until intercourse takes place. So in that moment of consummation the old covenant breaks. At that moment (underline the word **moment),** it is my belief, following the summation of the principles, that both former spouses have just committed the act of adultery against each other.

Also, to further reiterate this point that the new marriages do not automatically make the couples become one flesh , the charge of adultery cannot be applied, just because they remarried. If they live for the rest of their lives in their new unions without consummating those relationships, no adultery would have been committed, until that moment of consummation. Let us mirror the message of the exception clause by using **St. Mark 10: 11 & 12:**

11 And he saith unto them, Whosoever shall put away his wife, and marry another, committeth adultery against her.

12 And if a woman shall put away her husband, and be married to another, she committeth adultery.

So, because we see here that, with consideration to this particular circumstance, a legal remarriage in the natural realm by itself does not automatically make it become adultery until sex is initiated, then the term "marrieth another" here is referring to the spiritual remarriage, which is sexual intercourse, which the persons can engage in with or without being legally married.

However, in the case of the couples becoming legally married in the natural, God afterwards returns and (unlike if they were not legally remarried and was living in a common-law relationship, which would then become a fornicating lifestyle) blesses the new union, just because they are legally married. Because both the natural and the spiritual legal requirements have been met.

So we see that King James' version usage of the word married in this particular scripture isn't referring to a legal remarriage. It's speaking about the woman giving herself sexually to another man (according to Holman Christian Standard Bible). Therefore, she is "joined" to that other man as one flesh (according to New American Standard) because of sex. So then, the scriptures do not mean that being now legally remarried they would for the rest of their lives be called adulterers.

The only way that woman (and the same would go for the man) would continuously be called an adulteress is if she continues to have relations with that other person and have not **legally divorced** her rightful husband. If she stopped having sex with her husband and is only having intercourse with this other person, though not legally divorced in the natural, the spirit realm now recognizes her and her husband as being spiritually divorced, and a new illegal one-ness of flesh has been put in motion through the act of adultery. She creates confusion in the spirit, however, if she is having sex with both her husband and her lover. She would be continually making and breaking covenants between the two. So the point is, it is this kind of scenario, wherein, as long as she remains in it, that would make her be called an adulteress for the rest of her life.

When Jesus addressed the Samaritan woman at the well, He said: *"…go call thy husband…" She responded that 'she had no husband.' Jesus then said "Thou hast well said, I have no husband: For thou hast had five husbands; and he whom thou now hast is not thy husband: in that saidst thou truly (St. John 4: 16 – 18)"*

Whether she was legally married five times or not is not clear here. However, one thing is clear, the sixth man that she had was not a legal marriage in the natural and that is why she said I have no husband – I have no lawful husband! Curiously, though Jesus acknowledged that he was not her legal husband, He had referred to the man as her husband nonetheless, when He commanded her to go for Him. Jesus here used the term "husband" because in truth, though they were not legally married, they were one flesh in the spiritual realm through sexual intercourse. So spiritually he was her husband, but it was an illegal one-ness.

CHAPTER 5: IF DIVORCED ARE YOU CONDEMNED TO LIVE SINGLE?

So now, with Jesus' utterance at **St. Matthew 19:9:** *"...Whosoever shall put away his wife, except it be for fornication, and shall marry another, committeth adultery: and whoso marrieth her which is put away doth commit adultery."* Immediately In the following verse *"His disciples say unto him, If the case of the man be so with his wife, it is not good to marry".*

Even though they were now followers of Christ, the disciples had been weaned into, and therefore, was still influenced by a culture whereby a divorce was enacted for almost any reason. The people used the written Bill of divorcement frivolously as if Moses had created the law as a license for them to divorce. Therefore, when

Jesus stated that 'according to the spiritual principles of what makes and breaks the covenant, which is what would determine in the aftermath, the spiritual legality of a remarriage without carrying the charge of adultery, they despaired and said, 'well if that be the case, might as well stay unmarried.' To this, they were speaking of the Eunuch lifestyle.

Here, maybe they thought that Jesus would have commended them as some religious folks of today would do and say, 'how noble of you all to say this. Heaven would be so happy if you just never marry and make yourselves eunuchs for God.' And if you were married and got divorced or executed a divorce, 'how noble to stay single for the rest of your life and concentrate on God.' After all, even Paul said in **1 Corinthians 7:27** – *"…Art thou loosed from a wife? seek not a wife."*

But, surprisingly Jesus did not dole out any such commendation. Instead, he said, not everyone can live the life of a eunuch. He named three categories of eunuchs, but in a fourth category Jesus placed those persons who were not given that gift:

"But he said unto them, all men cannot receive this saying, save they to whom it is given.

¹² For there are some eunuchs, which were so born from their mother's womb: and there are some eunuchs, which were made eunuchs of men: and there be eunuchs, which have made themselves eunuchs for the kingdom of heaven's sake. He that is able to receive it, let him receive it (St. Matthew 19:11 & 12).

In that exception clause, Jesus is explicitly saying that Heaven expects that you will remarry if you are divorced and the portion of a eunuch is not yours to take. Jesus is not endorsing divorce, but He understands and accepts that if you were not given the ability to stay single, then you will not be expected to stay single. You will have to remarry. Also, once again let me declare, Jesus did not put forward the exception clause because of the pain the cheated must feel if infidelity had occurred. He was merely conceding to the pre-ordained principles of what makes the man and woman become one flesh and the principles that can break that covenant. Again, all other reasons that one might divorce for are peripherals and are weak to what indeed can break the agreement in the spirit realm – sex! Hence the exception clause!

About Paul saying: *"…Art thou loosed from a wife? Seek not a wife (1 Corinthinans 7:27)."* this would seem to agree with the disciples and seem to be contradicting Jesus. But no. He was not preventing anyone from getting married. Earlier on in the **1 Corinthians chapter 7 at verses 7 – 9**, he was basically saying that 'if one can receive the eunuch lifestyle and remain single, that would be great because that person could concentrate more on the Lord without distraction.' However, he acknowledged that not everyone had that "gift" to live that way, just as Jesus acknowledged that too, so in such a case, it is better to marry than to burn:

"For I would that all men were even as I myself. But every man hath his proper gift of God, one after this manner, and another after that.

I say therefore to the unmarried and widows, It is good for them if they abide even as I. But if they cannot contain, let them marry: for it is better to marry than to burn."

In **1 Timothy 4:3** Paul rebukes those who were preventing persons from getting married. So if you happen to be divorced, cannot contain yourself and it's not possible to remarry your ex, it is better to go and get married, but only to someone who is in the faith like yourself **(1 Corinthians 7:39)**. Of course, Paul, right here at verse 39, was talking specifically about the covenant being severed by death, but the same advice holds true for anyone who is divorced or who divorces because the bond was cut due to infidelity. Also, by the same token, if it was not because of adultery and remarriage occurs, in the end, Grace will still appear to make it become acceptable before God.

**** Further to 1 Corinthians 7, verses 27 says that 'if we are married, we should not seek to get divorced, but if we have become divorced (your partner could enact it, ev-en though you don't believe in it), we should stay single."

Paul gave this advice, not because he was against the order of marriage, but Paul's personal opinion was that a person who can control their urges would serve GOD better being single, but he always quickly comes out of his personal reverie and offer a proper balance to alleviate any misunderstanding. Hence in verse 28 he went on to say that 'if the divorcee remarries (this does not differentiate from whether the marriage had ended through infidelity or not), that person would not have committed any sin to remarry.' And he also added that 'if a virgin marries, that person also, would not be wrong to do so.'

**** This content added for third publication

CHAPTER 6: WHAT IF YOU ARE DIVORCED MULTIPLE TIMES?

*T*he answer is simple: ***The same path that a spring finds to flow, is the same path that a river can go.***

If Grace forgave and restored you to a rightful standing with God after a divorce and remarriage in observance of the principles laid down, then the number of times that one is divorced does not matter. Grace can still be called upon for another renewal.

By now I am sure that my readers have gotten the message that the purpose of this book is not to promote divorce. Neither is it saying that God supports it. While God does not want us to take His Grace for granted and as a license to sin (because He is not the minister of sin), equally, He does not want us to wallow in ignorance. He wants us to serve Him intelligently, with proper knowledge **(Psalms 47:7)**.

Myself have been married and divorced three times. Yes. You read it correctly. Three times! I am not proud of this. I cringe every time I say it. But it is what it is, and all I can say is, thank God for Grace.

God never told me to get a divorce. I made those decisions based on the issues that I was faced with. People who are religious and who walk in blind faith have been quick to point the finger at me but God is a just God! Just as how He did not place liability on Moses for enacting a divorce law, God understands that while – get this – while it is a fact that in all three marriages I most certainly had faults too, the righteous God does not heap all the blame on me. He rightly divides accountability. I would have preferred never to have experienced the pain of a divorce, much more three, but the final decisions were reached, because of decisions that the other parties had themselves made as well.

On the point of my having been divorced three times, at one point I had an interesting conversation with a Pastor. It was evident that he had disdain for my having been a three-time divorcee. I took him to Bible school. I said, 'man of God if you berate me for having been divorced three times, I am going to shock the socks off of you. In truth, I had been married and divorced many more times than three times.' He looked bewildered.

I went through the whole thing about what makes and breaks the covenant, because that is the principal thing that must be understood. I said, here is the shocker: 'let's say, for example, that throughout my life, I have had sex (apart from my three legal marriages), with twenty women. Having not cheated on my last wife and having not slept with another woman since we got divorced, our covenant is still intact, though we are legally divorced (that is, of course, if she herself has not been with another man before or after our divorce). Therefore, over the course of my life, I have been spiritually married and divorced twenty-two times between my illegal intercourses and my two failed marriages, before the third and last marriage. The day that I have sex with another woman or her with another man that is the day that my third wife and I would be spiritually divorced, just as how we are presently now legally divorced in the natural. So as it stands now, using this figure as an example, I have been divorced twenty-two times as opposed to the three times that you thought I was guilty of. What do you think of me now?'

To further drive home the point I asked, "Pastor, is your wife the only woman that you have ever had?" He began to get defensive and started to say that he had never cheated on his wife. I said, "Sir, I never asked if you had cheated on your wife, I meant if she was the only woman that you have ever known intimately. You were not born saved, and you must have had a few romps in the sack before you got saved.' He finally conceded that 'he was not a virgin when he got married.' So with a straight face, I said, 'Sir, you too are guilty of having been divorced several times. Though you were not legally married to any of those women during your playboy days, by sexual intercourse, you became spiritually married, and each time you left the one and started a sexual relationship with someone else you spiritually divorced the former lover and had established a new covenant with your new lover.

So, man of God, if Grace had imparted forgiveness and restoration to you for all those divorces and God now recognizes you in your present union, then the same principles for forgiveness and restoration have been afforded to me as well. Matters not how many times I had walked the path. Grace that was valid the first time is still valid for all those other times.'

He looked at me as if he was just shocked out of a stupor. Maybe he was.

Everyone Is Guilty of Being a Divorcee!

Some, like my good friend, the Minister, have looked down on me with scorn because I have been divorced three times. From a human perspective, this is understandable, but every one of us who have, over the period of our lives, been in more than one intimate relationship is guilty of a divorce. So, therefore, hardly anyone can condemn me for being a divorcee, albeit three times.

Many will say, but a common-law relationship is different from a legal marriage.

There is no difference, except that one is legal before God and man, and the other is not. Each of them nonetheless, was consummated through sexual intercourse, thus making both relationships of one flesh. Therefore, they are spiritually married. When they move on to have sex with someone else, they bring about a spiritual divorce and have consummated a new spiritual marriage. And so forth.

The same principles that are necessary to keep a marriage together are the very same principles that are needed to keep a common-law relationship together. Some persons have had excellent long-term common-law relationships because they followed the policies that kept their relationship fruitful. Need I say that I am not endorsing a fornicating union? I am not. I am merely pointing out the fact that there are principles to follow for a good relationship, then there are principles, that, if followed, will guarantee a lousy relationship, be it a legal union or a common-law one.

Then there are those who are legally married, and the relationship breaks down to the point of divorce, just because that couple, though legally bound did not continue to apply the principles that would have ensured longevity for the marriage. Of which I too, have been guilty. Hence I have been legally married and divorced three times, but illegally married and divorced many more times than that.

Then there is the issue of one being made dumb in the church because one remarries. That minister or those ministers of that denomination heartily crucify the innocent, ignorantly thinking that they are championing the cause for righteousness.

Divorcee? Backbench!

Some churches unceremoniously punish you to backbench if you are unfortunate enough to be a divorcee and remarry, yet amongst those leaders, there might be some who are guilty of having slept with or is sleeping with a church sister or just another woman.

While they reproach and banish the member who has divorced and remarried, little do they know that they too are guilty of the very same crime, so they too should be compelled to sit at the back of the congregation. In like manner, the "Far-to-sees and the Sad-to-sees" were priding themselves on not committing fornication and adultery because they never physically committed the act. But Jesus said that 'the act is born first within the heart. Therefore, though they might not have done it they were still guilty if they lusted.'

As I have been saying, sexual intercourse creates the spiritual bond called oneness of flesh. This is marriage, spiritually. Equally, when that minister sleeps with the church sister he has spiritually divorced his wife and has established a new covenant spiritually with his concubine, just like Bathsheba did when she slept with David. And the point have already been made that the spiritual realm has to recognize and acknowledge the one-ness made, and the covenant that is broken as such, not because God is in agreement with sin but due to the laid down principles of God for what makes and breaks the covenant spiritually. And because this concubinage situation has not come into legal marriage, it is an illegal one-ness, which causes it to become sin.

Each time that minister goes home and sleeps with his wife he re-establishes the covenant. So if he continues to go back and forth between his wife and his concubine (s) he creates confusion of spirit. He is continually divorcing and remarrying. Backbench!

Jesus does not reveal these truths to embarrass us. He wants us to realize that we just cannot keep His laws blamelessly and also for us to appreciate the fact that He came to be our righteousness. Many times when we think that we stand, we fall. Therefore, we must be less judgemental and more merciful. **Galatians 6: 1 – 3** encourages us:

" Brethren, if a man be overtaken in a fault, ye which are spiritual, restore

such an one in the spirit of meekness; considering thyself, lest thou also be tempted.

Bear ye one another's burdens, and so fulfill the law of Christ.

For if a man think himself to be something, when he is nothing, he deceiveth himself."

We must never condone sin. We must, however, always be of a mind to restore. If God had said: one who divorces and remarries will never be forgiven and be recognized in that new union, then so be it. We could never receive such a case. Therefore, backbench would have been appropriate. But God never said that. Traditionally, we have read the surface of the written word but have never allowed the Holy Spirit to make that written word become the Living Word (which is Christ) within us. Therefore, we do not have the mind of Christ on too many things. Hence, we create doctrines and place people and ourselves under yokes that God never ordained.

Different denominations have their church doctrines. God is a God of order. Therefore, if you agree to become a member of their church, you are expected to abide by their house rules. And indeed so, that there be no confusion within the house of God. To keep order and to honour the fact that the religious leaders sat in the God-ordained office of the Priesthood, Jesus admonished His listeners:

"All therefore whatsoever they bid you observe, that observe and do; but do not ye after their works: for they say, and do not." - **St. Matthew 23:3.**

Church leaders must be honoured and respected doubly if they serve well **(1 Timothy 5:17)** but if not we must still honour the office that they hold, because it was ordained by God Himself. Leaders therefore, must be mindful to ensure that the laws they impose must bear, not only the written word but its God-intended meaning. Otherwise, it's useless.

Jesus said that 'the Pharisees and the Sadducees were worshipping God in vain because they watered down – changed the true meaning of God's doctrines and introduced them to the people. Thus, in the spiritual realm, their words could not be moved to any divine manifestation. Thus, no one got any benefit and God got no glory. You see, God only moves on the volition of His own words, **with His intended meanings**, Just as how He hears and answers every prayer, but according to His will. When God said 'do not add or take away from My words' in **Revelation 22: 18 & 19** He was not mincing words when He said:

"I testify to everyone who hears the words of prophecy in this book: If anyone adds to them, God will add to him the plagues described in this book.

And if anyone takes away from the words of this book of prophecy, God will take away his share in the tree of life and in the holy city, which are described in this book."

Adding or taking away from His words isn't necessarily speaking about word usage. Different words can be used to explain scripture, in the same way that parallel translations show us, but as long as God's intended meaning is not shifted or twisted.

Chapter 7: WHAT DOES "THE HARDNESS OF YOUR HEARTS" MEAN?

"*T*he Pharisees also came unto him, tempting him, and saying unto him, Is it lawful for a man to put away his wife for every cause?

⁴ And he answered and said unto them, Have ye not read, that he which made them at the beginning made them male and female,

⁵ And said, For this cause shall a man leave father and mother, and shall cleave to his wife: and they twain shall be one flesh?

⁶ Wherefore they are no more twain, but one flesh. What therefore God hath joined together, let not man put asunder.

⁷ They say unto him, Why did Moses then command to give a writing of divorcement, and to put her away?

⁸ He saith unto them, Moses because of the hardness of your hearts suffered you to put away your wives: but from the beginning it was not so."- St. Matthew 19: 3 – 8.

When Jesus said that 'Moses allowed them to divorce their wives because of the hardness of their hearts', was Jesus saying that whenever a divorce happens, it is because unforgiveness and bitterness is always the case? No. I do not believe so. That was what I blindly thought, but as I peered more closely into the word I saw a deeper meaning.

It is true that some divorces come about because of unforgiveness, bitterness, hatred, you name it. However, I believe that Jesus was also making an inference to something else, because there are times when one is forced to divorce, due to the unacceptable behaviour of their spouse, and not because it is something that they relish or want to do, just as how Moses enacted the divorce law, but it was not an indication that he endorsed or supported it in any way. Circumstances and history can also reveal scripture. So let's peek at the divorce culture in Israel up to the time of Jesus coming on the scene to understand this deeper meaning.

The divorce dilemma never began in Israel because Moses created the divorce law. The divorce law was created because, not only were they already divorcing their wives but it was happening, and at an alarmingly high and foolish rate, in that, a man would divorce his wife for the most frivolous of reasons. But all this was being done verbally – by word of mouth. Therefore, apart from the fact that there were cases of unwillingness to forgive, this ability to divorce by word of mouth was obviously creating another huge problem. There is a saying: my word is my bond. And indeed it should be. Hence Jesus said, "let your yes be yes, and your no be no." However, not every man is noble. Therefore, in many instances a man would verbally divorce his wife and then if it suits his purpose, if she is caught with another man, for example, he would lie that he had divorced her. Thus causing her and her new lover to be stoned to death according to Moses' law in **Leviticus 20:10**. He could be so cruel for any number of reasons. Even though he had chased her away, maybe he became jealous of knowing that she went to another man and out of jealous rage, reneged on the divorce agreement or utterance. That is wickedness to the highest degree which spirals out of the hardness of one's heart.

The scriptures never said as much. How then did I come by this truth? Simple. The word of God declares that 'we are all men of like or similar passions or faults. **St. James 5:17** refers to Elijah as *"...a man subject to like passions as we are..."* Paul and Barnabas in **Acts 14:15**, to prevent the people from worshipping them after a lame man was healed through them said*: "...Sirs, why do ye these things? We also are men of like passions with you..."*

Ecclesiastes 1:9 says: *"What has been will be again. What has been done, will be done again; there is nothing new under the sun."*Therefore, when I look around me and see the flawed character of myself and my fellow man I realise that in the absence of written proof, unscrupulous husbands would undoubtedly have been doing things like this to their hapless wives. So to prevent this evil from continuing, Moses had to do something about it. Thus he created the law that if a person is divorcing, or has been given a divorce, it must be presented in written form as proof to prevent the man from lying and from the innocent woman getting stoned to death.

The Woman Caught In The Act of Adultery

For a classic example of the hardness of their hearts and also of their twisting and watering down scriptures to suit themselves, let's go to **St. John 8; 1 – 5:**

"Jesus went unto the mount of Olives.

² And early in the morning he came again into the temple, and all the people came unto him; and he sat down, and taught them.

³ And the scribes and Pharisees brought unto him a woman taken in adultery; and when they had set her in the midst,

⁴ They say unto him, Master, this woman was taken in adultery, in the very act.

⁵ Now Moses in the law commanded us, that such should be stoned: but what sayest thou?"

Moses' law in **Leviticus 20: 10** says:

"And the man that committeth adultery with another man`s wife, even he that committeth adultery with his neighbour›s wife, the adulterer and the adulteress shall surely be put to death."

The religious leaders. Get this – not any member of the common populace, but the religious leaders - those who were masters in Israel, brought the woman to Jesus, stating that 'she was caught in the very act of adultery.' The woman did not commit adultery by herself. There had to have been a man involved, and Moses' law commanded that the man also should be brought forth, and that 'both he and the woman should be stoned to death.' I find it interesting that in this verse of scripture it did not mention the woman first, but the man – *"the man that committeth adultery with another man's wife…"* And yet, curiously, the woman was brought forward to be killed, but the man was nowhere to be found. The leaders were undeniably breaking the scriptures by declaring that the woman was to be stoned to death, yet give the man a free pardon.

The hardness of their hearts could be said to be manifesting here as well, in that, as we know it, society is more tolerant of a man's infidelity than that of a woman's so naturally, society is quicker to call for the woman's blood than for the man's own.

Thank God Jesus was there that day. However, let me point out that Jesus never gave that woman a free pardon. If He had done that He too would have been guilty of breaking His scriptures. He let her go because He had come to take those stones for her at Calvary. The word of God said that 'the soul that sinneth shall die' and Jesus had come to die in her stead.

The purpose of His mission is also the reason why, when James and John, the sons of thunder, or short-tempered ones wanted Jesus to call down fire and brimstone on

some who did not receive Him, the Lord rebuked them and said: *"you do not know what spirit ye are of."* - **St. Luke 9:55.** Indeed it is true that Elijah had commanded fire upon some whom idolatrous King Ahaziah had sent to him. They all were idol worshippers and deserved to die. It's quite evident that God agreed with Elijah; hence the fire came. So now, why is Jesus rebuking His disciples for suggesting that He come in agreement to repeat this punishment? Simple. Just like His reasons for sparing the adulterous woman, Jesus was not giving them a free pardon. He had come to die the death of their disobedience and rejection of Himself.

CHAPTER 8: DIVORCED AND REMARRIED BUT STILL NOT FREE!

*I*n any conversation about divorce and remarriage, many who had grown up under the tutelage of traditional church doctrine, whether they are still saved or not will inadvertently utter the words: "I don't believe in divorce and remarriage." Sometimes one could hear the automation in their voices. They utter the words, but the sound is empty – there is no real conviction there. It's as if they are just dragging that line along, not because they genuinely believe in the merit of their utterance. They mindlessly, blindly just hold on to that so-called belief, all because it was part of their customary teachings growing up, and not because they have come to the knowledge of that in which they believed. When God calls us to Himself, He instructs us to believe in Him. However, he does not expect us to stay on the knoll of belief forever. He expects us to graduate from merely believing, and come into the knowledge of Himself. Why?

You see, on "Belief Hill" you will not only find Christians there but non-Christians as well. On Belief Hill you will find, not just those who believe in Jesus, but those who believe only in God and not Jesus, those who believe in other gods, and those who believe that there is no God. But God is always raising the bar and sets Himself at higher standards than anything or anyone else. Therefore, He goes about to prove Himself to His people. The other gods cannot do this, because they are no gods, but just the figment of their worshippers' imagination. Just like Elijah and the Baal prophets. Both Elijah and the false prophets had their own belief about whom God was. Baal could not have brought his followers into the knowledge of himself because he just does not exist but Jehovah God, on the other hand, is the First and the Last; the Everlasting and All-mighty One. He was able to prove Himself and thus further graduated Elijah from merely believing and into the knowledge of Himself. The Baal prophets, on the other hand, got a rude awakening!

Paul the Apostle, when he persecuted the church, it wasn't because he hated God. He believed in God. He just did not know Him. But after Jesus introduced Himself and began to deal with him, at another place and time Paul returned and testified: **'for I now know Him in Whom I had believed and I am now convinced that He is able…' – 2 Timothy 1:12**

The irony, the hypocrisy and the tragedy of this mindless utterance of belief of not believing in divorce and remarriage, is that, put together, they all fall into the category of either backslider living in common-law relationships; those who are still saved but single, or of those living in a dead marriage, but think that they can't escape. Let's look at each of these:

The Back-sliders!

These people either grew up in the church, and had been indoctrinated into that belief, or they were once saved but have since gone back out into the world of sin. They are involved in a common-law relationship, and they would say things like: 'I know that I am not where I am supposed to be in the Lord but I don't believe in divorce and remarriage, that's why I am not rushing into marriage. I am taking my time.' Taking what time? That's a lie! One cannot be intimately involved with someone and at the same time state that 'you are not rushing into marriage.'

To take your time or to wait, means that you are free, single and not intimately involved. Perhaps these persons are fooling themselves into thinking that God won't be so angry with them for living outside of His will if they testify that they do not believe in divorce and remarriage. The point is, you are already married, spiritually through sex with that person with whom you are intimate. But it is an illegal one-ness called fornication. Hence God is saying: "**⁴ Marriage is honourable in** *all, and the bed undefiled: but whoremongers and adulterers God will judge." – Hebrews 13:4.* Therefore, these hypocrites need to get out of their twisted stupor and get it right with God. If two persons see enough in each other to be subjecting themselves to a sexual relationship with each other, then they can get married. One cannot just wish that they never get divorced. To avoid such a misfortune, you both, equally have to put in the work to ensure that divorce does not appear at your door. Additionally, and especially for women, it is entirely unfair to the one who will one day wind up to be your spouse, for you to waste your lives with someone or with several other men for years, while you are "waiting" for the right man to come and marry you. When Mr Right finally appears, what does he get: a woman whose body is tired from all the kids she has had for other men and from the other rigours of past relationships. She just wants to retire on Mr Right. Wasted years!

The Saved, But Single!

The people in this category never tasted marital bliss, and subsequently have never been bitten by the divorce bug. Therefore, their belief system is based on erroneous church doctrine and pure conjecture – un-tested, unsubstantiated belief at best!

The Married, But Not Married!

The people in this category, saved or not, are married, but the marriage has died. However, years roll on and they still remain officially married even though the embers have gone cold and there are no sparks.

The unsaved ones stay together, even though they are not still together, because they fear that if they divorce and remarry, God would never forgive them and would send them to hell. The irony, the hypocrisy and the tragedy in this is that one or both of them usually are involved with someone else, but they won't divorce because they "fear God." Need I say again that they are already spiritually divorced from their spouse and have become spiritually married to the person with whom they are cheating? Then if they keep coming home to still sleep with each other, they create confusion of spirit because they both keep making and breaking the covenant between themselves.

The saved ones, just like the unsaved married couple, remain together even though their marriage is dead, for the same reason of thinking that if they divorce they would be sent to a hopeless hell. And somehow, they fool themselves into thinking that if they endure the lifeless marriage, God is carving out some special reward in Heaven for their "faithfulness." What baloney! If they were that faithful to God they would both determine to make the marriage work. The marriage is not working because of unfaithfulness to God and to each other. I know. I have been there!

Divorced And Remarried – Yikes!

Then there is another unbelievable tragedy! Those who "do not believe in divorce and remarriage, but at some point in their lives, find themselves sitting on the divorce block! I can certainly relate to how that feels. I have been there - three times! One is overwhelmed by a complex array of emotions – regret, anger, bitterness, confusion, an immense feeling of failure, etc.

Christian women especially, being under the influence of their wrongful belief system that they cannot now remarry after a divorce, prepare themselves to become eunuchs to God for the rest of their lives. So they settle in, some even getting more deeply involved in ministry.

After a while, maybe a year, a couple of years or a few years have passed. The divorce dust has settled. Suddenly the divorcee begins to feel the urge for companionship. Sexual urges begin to re-emerge and become stronger. This usually would have proven to be the case for the man long before the woman starts to be thus affected.

Eventually, not only did the unthinkable - a divorce occurred in their lives, but now they have remarried, and their first spouse still lives.

These remarry, defying all that they had believed in, not because they have come into the KNOWLEDGE of truth that God would restore them in a remarriage, but because their human cravings were not entering into agreement with their belief system, and so they remarry. However, the tragedy is that, because they have still not come into spiritual knowledge on the matter, they live the rest of their newly wedded lives, not in marital bliss, but in an agonizing twist – they are married, but they are living under condemnation because they think that God is going to send them to hell.

To this God cries out – "My people are destroyed from lack of knowledge!"

Edward Vlll King of England lost his throne in 1936 due the nation's and the church's lack of knowledge in this respect.

Equally, Princess Margaret, the Queen's sister, wanted to marry her divorced lover. She was not permitted to do so and her life never seemed to settle to any true semblance of peaceful order after that. Lack of knowledge crushed the destiny of a king and probably marred the life of the beautiful princess, spiralling her into a downward lifestyle trend afterwards.

Even today, many are being ostracized because of church doctrine, and criticized by church folks for having been divorced and remarried. But *'He that the Son has set free is free indeed* (St. John 8:36).'

CHAPTER 9: THIS DIVORCE MADNESS MUST STOP!

*J*ust like in the days of Moses and Jesus, the divorce faucet, in this our day, has been turned on full force. The divorce rate both in and out of the church has reached phenomenal proportions. Something has to be done to stop this river of pain. But what can we do?

Go back to basics – back to the old landmark – back to listening to, embracing and putting in practice, God's appointed principles if we want marital success.

Too many of us after having learned, have turned away our hearts from following God's teachings and His pleadings. We have become fleshly, even though we still say Lord, Lord! And we know that the flesh is not subject to God or the things of God and neither can be. To the flesh God's ways are boring, just like good medicine is considered too bitter to take, but once applied, it brings forth good health. Likewise, the words and ways of God bring forth good spiritual health and well-being. To correct this crisis, however, it is going to be a tall task. The adage prevention is better than a cure could not be more true, in the face of this divorce dilemma. How though, can this situation be remedied?

From time to time churches hold brief singles and marriage seminars or conferences. For those expecting to get married, the Pastor would have a two-week pre-marital counselling session. All of this is good but it is not effective anymore. The relationship and divorce crisis have become too severe and have gone way out of proportion.

I said relationship and divorce here because the divorce rate has gone too high because of unresolved issues in relations and then there are those relationships that have not ended in official divorce, but too many are a facade. A pretense. Oh! The storms that rage and the contrary winds that blow behind closed doors! And we are Christians! This is a disgrace!

Turn Pre and Post-Marital Counselling Into Full Time Ministries

Instead of just having one day, a-few-days conferences, and a few sessions before marriage, in the same manner that churches have Bible Study and Sunday School ministries, there must now be a wholesome, on-going pre-marital, and post-marital ministry. That is, round-the-clock, in-depth, comprehensive nurturing in these areas, with adequately qualified, anointed, and dedicated ministerial teachers, and in as much as Wednesday night bible study and Sunday School are now a culture within the church, this new ministry must take on the image of that of a culture as well.

1. **What Will On-Going Pre-Marital Ministry Achieve?**

Not only will it better prepare our singles, both men and women for the order of marriage, which will lessen the chance of a divorce, but it being such an on-going ministry, will reawaken the nobility of marriage, and thus we will begin to see more people getting married within the church. You see, equally as the divorce rate has soared, in like manner the frequency of people getting married within the church has declined significantly. People are scared because, by the statistics, relationships are just not working anymore. But while nuptials are not so frequent anymore, flip-side is that sexual immorality has gained pre-eminence within the church. The fear that people have of getting married does not diminish or demolish natural sexual urges. So without one having their own husband or wife, fornication is bound to become an issue.

2. What Will On-Going Post Marital Ministry Achieve?

It will keep the nobility of marriage charged up!

To begin to stem the flow of divorce, attention needs to be paid to the foundation upon which the relationship is built. If the relationship is established upon breaking God's laws, there will be no trust, no respect and without these two there is no relationship.

Once the marital relationship is established, there is a hierarchy of the union that God Himself has developed and which must be observed and practised for the marriage to have success. Namely, Head of the household, the wife being subjected to her husband and children being in obedience to their parents. Let's look at them individually:

a). Head Of The Household!

By their actions, most men seem to think that "Head of the household" means that they are the only voice within the relationship – that they are the monarch, and everyone else bows and complies without question! This perception is so wrong. It is not the scriptural definition for the head of the household.

For us to even begin to understand this concept, let's look at Jesus Christ Who is the Head of His household, the Church, which is His bride. How does Jesus Christ our Lord execute His position as Head of His Church? Let's go to **Ephesians 5: 22 – 24:**

[22] *"Wives, submit yourselves unto your own husbands, as unto the Lord.*

[23] *For the husband is the head of the wife, even as Christ is the head of the church: and he is the saviour of the body.*

[24] *Therefore as the church is subject unto Christ, so let the wives be to their own husbands in everything."*

In exerting Himself in His household, Jesus Christ our Lord never doles out commands, rules and regulations from a selfish motives. He does so for our benefit. Period! Once more let's peek at **Hebrews 12: 9 & 10:**

"9Furthermore we have had fathers of our flesh which corrected us, and we gave them reverence: shall we not much rather be in subjection unto the Father of spirits, and live?

10For they verily for a few days chastened us after their own pleasure; but he for our profit, that we might be partakers of his holiness." Do you see it? Verse ten says Jesus does whatever "…for our profit…" Not from selfish motives.

Every command, rule and regulation is sent forth to make us better in mind, body, soul, spirit, finances and to make us excel in every other good thing. As the Head of His household, Jesus also leads by example. He is the Priest of His house. He protects, and He provides.

Now that we have a clear picture of how Christ operates as Head of His household, the image is equally now clear as to what the husband's role in the home should be. Any well thinking woman would want to submit to that. Speaking of which, let's look at the meaning of the wife submitting herself to her husband.

b). Wives Subject yourself to your husband

[22]*"Wives, submit yourselves unto your own husbands…" – Hebrews 5:22*

Due to the wrong concept that most men seem to have, with regards to their role as head of the household, some women cringe at this, and every other scripture that commands them to submit to their husbands. The wrongful thinking husband here believes that submission means that she must make herself a floor mat to be trampled on. However, this way of thinking is so wrong. It is not the biblical definition of submission.

[24] **"Therefore as the church is subject unto Christ, so let the wives be to their own husbands in everything."** - *Hebrews 5:24*

Submission or subjection here means to come in agreement with – the wife must come in agreement with her husband in all things. It does not mean all things as in, if the husband wants to lead the wife away from the commandments of God, that she should obey that. Nonetheless, even in the wife not subjecting herself to her husband wanting her to stray from God in any way, there is a wrong and a right way to deal with this problem (this will be dealt with shortly). The verse right here speaks to the premise that the husband is executing well his role as head of the household, according to Jesus' instructions. She should not circumvent or side-step that. To disagree with a man who is subjecting himself to the Head of his life, which is Christ, is to be in open rebellion to God.

If the husband is subjected to Christ the Head of his life, he will be in line with God. Thus the wife is instructed to come into agreement with that.

How To Deal With Wrongful Submission Expectations

1 Corinthians 7:5 King James Version (KJV) declares: *"Defraud ye not one the other, except it be with consent for a time, that ye may give yourselves to fasting and prayer; and come together again, that Satan tempt you not for your incontinency."*

Contemporary English Version (CEV) explains it like this: *"So don't refuse sex to each other, unless you agree not to have sex for a little while, in order to spend time in prayer. Then Satan won't be able to tempt you because of your lack of self-control."*

Fasting and prayer are essential to our Christian walk. In **St. Matthew 17:21** Our Lord Jesus Christ instructs us to fast.

Scenario – 1 Corinthians 7:5 makes it very clear that 'neither the husband or the wife should embark on fasting without first coming into an agreement.' However, let us say that the husband never wants to fast, but instead he wants to have sex every night. The husband right here is not being a good head of the home. He is the priest of the household, as such, he should be leading the family to worship. But now he is not. Because he is not at that moment, being compliant with Jesus, the Head of his life, should the wife disobey her husband to go fast and pray?

The wife is now in a dilemma. Her husband, whom God had instructed her to be in subjection to, at this point is wanting her to subject to a directive that is against an instruction of God. She needs to be obedient to God, but at the same time, she needs to keep the harmony of her home. Peace must be pursued but never at the expense of disobeying God. Herein is wisdom like that of Abigail **in 1 Samuels 25.** *She "…was a woman of good understanding, and of a beautiful countenance…"* who wisely averted David's wrath against her "churlish" husband.

The wife should humbly and respectfully let it be clear to her husband that she is not in agreement with her husband never allowing her time to fast. However, she should submit to his wishes for sex every night. Then in secret, she should make her complain to God. As sure as night follows day, after a while, the Lord will begin to work on his conscience. And he will repent of this evil. Even if he does not fast, he will eventually allow her time to fast.

If the wife, however, begins to be openly rebellious and go against the husband's wishes, thinking that God would be pleased, she is in for a rude awakening. Because she lets flesh get in the way, the Spirit of God cannot work. He does not operate in confusion. Therefore, the husband's heart could become hardened due to the wife's rigidity. Thus the situation becomes worse.

When The Wife Becomes Submissive, What Happens Next?

So to reiterate the principles of the marital hierarchy, it is:

1. The husband must first ensure that he is in submission to Jesus Christ, the Head of his life then take up his mantle as the head of his household.

2. The wife must be submissive or come in agreement with her husband in all things (which will be a joy if he is first submitted to God).

3. After the wife's submission **TO** her husband is established, it is then that the husband himself must now become submissive within the relationship **WITH** his wife. So it is submission **TO** and then submission **WITH**. This, in accordance with the directive at **Ephesians 5:21** which says: *"Submitting yourselves one to another in the fear of God."*

    This verse was not directed to married couples in particular. Paul was mainly talking about how we all should conduct ourselves as believers, and be in submission to each other. However, under the same principle of humility and brotherly love, the same can be aptly applied, even more so to married couples. Hence, this principle can and should apply to husbands with their wives.

The example of Jesus can also strengthen this viewpoint, when He Himself becomes subjected to the Heavenly Father after He has completed His task, mentioned here in **1 Corinthians 15: 24 – 28 :**

"[24] Then cometh the end, when He shall have delivered up the kingdom to God, even the Father; when He shall have put down all rule and all authority and power.

[25] For He must reign, till he hath put all enemies under His feet.

[26] The last enemy that shall be destroyed is death.

[27] For He hath put all things under His feet. But when He saith all things are put under Him, it is manifest that He is excepted, which did put all things under Him.

[28] And when all things shall be subdued unto Him, then shall the Son also himself be subject unto Him that put all things under Him, that God may be all in all."

Presently, the Father has given all power to Jesus Christ His Son to complete the redemption of humankind fully. Jesus made the declaration of His authority in **St. Matthew 28:21** by saying:

"All power is given unto Me in Heaven and on earth." Then there are other scriptures which point to this.

4. The family unit, however, cannot be complete without including the children of and within the union. They must be trained to be submissive to their parents. Once that is accomplished, just like the harmony which resides within the Trinity – God the Father, God the Son and God the Blessed Holy Spirit, you will have a perfect family unit made up of the father, mother and children.

Be Mindful of Whose Coverage You Go Under In Marriage

Now that we get an idea of what head of the household and what submission means, it is of utmost importance for sisters to be very careful as to whose covering they agree to come under in marriage for subjection. Once you are in it, you are expected to comply with it.

Often a Christian woman would disobey the word of God in **2 Corinthians 6:14** which explicitly commands:

"Be ye not unequally yoked together with unbelievers: for what fellowship hath righteousness with unrighteousness? and what communion hath light with darkness?"

They either do this out of frustration in not seeing any Christian suitors come their way, or because they like a particular guy, even though he is not a Christian. Most of them would encourage the man to "come to Church and get baptised". Not even properly and sincerely imploring him to give his life to Jesus Christ, but just to come to church to make it look good, so that they can get married. Even more so, if they had already begun to engage in sexual intercourse. Then when those rogue sisters get married to the unregenerate soul, and that person begins to go back to his beloved sin, those sisters will begin to clog up the altars, begging for prayers for their "bad" husbands. Huh?! Why would you be surprised? You got what you paid for! If the time-tested and enduring material of God's principles is not the foundation upon which that relationship is built, it is doomed to failure, unless repentance comes into play afterwards, and God decides to show great favour, and fix up what you messed up!

Build Your Relationship With Good Foundation

As mentioned just now, according to the word of God, if one person serves the Lord Jesus Christ and the other person does not, this presents an immediate disparity that is likely to cause all kinds of problems in the relationship. Therefore, this unequal yoke right here is a terrible foundation material with which to build your relationship.

An unequal union is not only relegated to Christian versus non-Christian (as in a sinner without God and Christ or no religion). Here are two other categories of an unequal union:

1. Christian is married to a person of a religious sect that does not honour and worship Jesus Christ as Lord and Saviour. Technically, that person is also a sinner without God and Christ for the Father said, if we do not honour the Son we have no lot nor part with Him, because **'there is no other name by which man can be saved, but by the name of Jesus Christ '– Acts 14:12**).

2. Christian is married to another Christian, but one who is of another denomination. Different denominations mean different doctrines, which sometimes could mean differences of opinions, that could have devastating consequences. Let me quickly point out though that if the two Christians are mature enough in their faith to know that it's not about the religion, but a relationship with Jesus Christ, and they feel comfortable with agreeing to disagree, it is a union that could work. But the rule of thumb is, differences of religious opinions could spell doom for a relationship.

Therefore, it is foolish to implement "unequal" as one of the foundation materials for your relationship. Other dissatisfactory foundation materials are:

1. **The practice of testing it before you rest in it.**
   While sex is vital in a relationship, society simply puts too much of a high rating on sex, hence the expectations are too much. Females especially are guilty of placing too much emphasis on that 'they want a man who can sweep them off their feet, take them continuously up to cloud nine,' but they never consider that they themselves cannot deliver that which they demand.

   This wrongful practice has caused many a sister, even after testing several brothers, and even men who are not Christians, to remain unmarried for years to come, though she might be beautiful and have all the hallmarks of a "nice Christian girl." Now she is not spoken for, because the guys who have had her think less of her, and true to form, they would not keep her secret. Typically, being men, they would feel compelled to publish their prowess. To deflower a Christian girl is juicy news.

2. **Refusing To Observe And Embrace God's Relationship Rules**

    God has laid down the blueprint for relationship success, like the role of each partner in the relationship. Each person embracing their part is good foundation material and also the element with which the couple must continue to build their relationship. If we do not practice these principles, we are doomed to fail in our marriages.

    In many instances, the roles have been reversed. The woman puts on the Britches. She becomes the man of the house, and the man, growing so emasculated, turns into a bumbling idiot of no consequence in the relationship. Some women will say that 'they had to assume the role, because the man was not stepping up.' We know that there are some of those types of men, but under no circumstance must a woman assume the role of head of household. No matter how lacking she might feel her husband to be, she must submit her will to God. As such, even if she has to tackle some tasks, she must never take the mantle. It's not yours, and God will judge you for that if you take it. Equally, if the man has the mantle, and does not utilise it properly, he will, in turn, have to answer to God for that. One cannot just assume the throne of a king simply because the king is not ruling well. One may advise, and support the king in every way, to enhance his kingship for his kingdom to thrive, but to assert one's self to the crown is treason, worthy of death.

Not rushing into a relationship has less to do with the observance of a time factor and more to do with how we approach and enter into the relationship. If a couple observes the rule of at least six months of dating, but they build on lies, deceit and with anything else that is less than God's standards for relationship success, they are still not ready to get married, even if they date for a year. However, if from the beginning of dating, sincerity, honesty, and respect for God's ordinances are fully applied, they might be ready for marriage even before six months.
For the divorce dilemma to be stanched, we must stop our mad rush into relationships with wrong motives and wrong principles.

We have strayed from God – from the core meanings of His laws. We have set them aside and have implemented our strategies by not building on the right foundation, and by not continuing to grow our marriages with the same excellent material that is used to produce a good foundation. Speaking of which, there are many things that can destroy a marriage, but one of the most notorious relationship killer is unfaithfulness. Let's go there.

CHAPTER 10:

A MARRIAGE SANCTIONED BY GOD CAN DIE!

*I*t is crucial not to let this slip: A couple might indeed build the relationship by adequately observing God's rules and regulations, gets the green light from God to go ahead, and afterwards begin to develop the marriage with lousy material. So even though God had initially permitted the union, because the couple did not continue in the same vein, the marriage can still end in divorce.

Some might disagree, saying that if God sanctions a marriage that it cannot go wrong, and end in divorce. They might argue that God would never have consented if He knew that in the end, the marriage would not work.

Was it not God Who had performed the first marriage ceremony? One could say that was a match made in Heaven. And it was. Creation was perfect. Adam was perfect. Eve was perfect - they were basking in the warmth of God's perfect will. But then the unthinkable happened – sin came in, and the marriage was in turmoil. To be honest, judging by our inherent human characteristics it is my personal belief that that marriage had initially ended, but then they came back together in union, maybe because there was not another woman for Adam to find. Look at it – one minute, and they were enjoying unparalleled bliss in a perfect paradise and the next minute, creation was plunged into the abyss of death. Less has broken up marriages, much more this. Losing paradise would indeed have dealt a telling blow to the relationship.

Can anyone then say that it wasn't God Who had created them, and had married them, because of the problems they brought upon their union, and upon creation? No. For a marriage to work, God will do His part, but then there is our part to play as well. If we do not execute our charge, we can end in divorce, even if God had originally sanctioned it. Equally, salvation has been made available to humankind, but the which cannot manifest to completion if man doesn't do his part, which is to accept and follow Jesus Christ to the end.

Unfaithfulness - The Notorious Killer!

Anything negative and unresolved can destroy a relationship, but there is one that sticks out like a sore thumb – infidelity – unfaithfulness – cheating! The choice of a name to call it cannot lessen its terrible impact.

From an emotional standpoint, the feeling of betrayal sometimes is beyond words. Trust is gone, and with it that sense of security. You built your world around someone, opening up entirely, surrendering your heart - you lay bare your vulnerability, soaring with trusting, carefree abandon up, up into the inviting arms of love, and then, heartbreak! Your upward flight is abruptly, cruelly disrupted, and suddenly, without warning you are plummeting headlong into a black abyss of unimaginable pain and desolation! Nonetheless, I will not dwell much longer on the emotional side of the dark effects of infidelity. For the purpose of this book, I will stick to the laws of its negative workings in the natural and in the spiritual.

Everything that we do in the natural, we give birth to something in the spiritual realm, which in turn comes back to negatively or positively affect us. The natural calls out to the spiritual, and the spiritual answers back. When Cain killed his brother, Abel, God said:

"…What hast thou done? the voice of thy brother's blood crieth unto me from the ground." – **Genesis 4:10.**

Whenever a couple is faithful to each other, their energies are focused. The intensity of the love is noticeable and can be easily felt. However, the minute the door of infidelity is opened up the commitment level begins to wane – the attention spool becomes less taut. It might not be very noticeable at first. The partner might not know right away what exactly is wrong, but the secrets are being unfolded in the supernatural. The ominous vibrations are there, crying out to our sub-conscious. God told Adam:

"...of the tree of the knowledge of good and evil, thou shalt not eat of it: for in the day that thou eatest thereof thou shalt surely die." **– Genesis 2:17.**

After Eve ate the fruit, and Adam saw that she did not keel over and die, and he looked around and saw that paradise looked just the same – everything around them was still breathtakingly beautiful. He must have thought that God was exaggerating, so he also took a bite. Little did he know that his wife's disobedience had already opened up a door, and the rumblings of doom were already heading towards them, as the Lord had warned. However, just as how Jesus, the second Adam is our covering, Adam was Eve's covering. Therefore, if he had not reciprocated her rebellion, his obedience would have averted the disaster and brought her back into proper relations with God. After all, he was the one who had received the commandment and not her. And also, the word of God says that because of the first Adam's disobedience, everyone died, and because of the second Adam's obedience, all are made righteous. It stands to reason then, that if the first Adam had remained in obedience, because he remained in his perfectness through obedience, God would have restored Eve. And everyone who came after would have been born righteous.

Just as Adam took his first bite, he immediately felt the shift – the robe of righteousness and perfectness that had covered them was instantly gone. The nakedness Adam felt was the spiritual disrobing. Wherein he was perfectly wise before, he now became disoriented, confused. He began to blame his natural nudity for his spiritual lacking. Their unfaithfulness to God had opened up an entrance in the supernatural realm, which gave birth to death and destruction. Paradise was lost! In this same manner, unfaithfulness opens up the door to the demise of the relationship. The bliss that was once enjoyed has become corrupted. Therefore, though it might seem like fun to do some discreet cheating now and again, the end of the matter will not be profitable. It will undoubtedly bring disaster.

I will Repay Your Unfaithfulness.

As mentioned earlier in the excerpt on the woman caught in the act of adultery, society has always been more tolerant of a man being promiscuous, than of a woman. Our culture seems to suggest that it is a manly thing for a man to be involved with more than one woman at the same time. Therefore, society expects this of him. Of course, it is wrong in God's sight. Once more let us borrow from **St. Matthew 19: 4 – 6:** *"And he answered and said unto them, Have ye not read, that he which made them at the beginning made them male and female,*

⁵ And said, For this cause shall a man leave father and mother, and shall cleave to his wife: and they twain shall be one flesh?

⁶ Wherefore they are no more twain, but one flesh. What therefore God hath joined together, let not man put asunder."

Jesus is very evidently saying that it is not multiple women with one's wife, but one woman to one man in a monogamous relationship for the rest of our lives.

Due to men's cheating ways, many women have now taken the position that they, out of spite, will begin to cheat as well. They have convinced themselves that revenge will be sweet. But they have not considered the end results. **Ecclesiastes 7:8** declares that *'the end of a matter is better than its beginning.'* In this instance it doesn't mean that this end will be sweet, but whatever we do the end consequence must always be considered.

The End Results Of Payback

It would do well for the woman to stop and consider that when she opens up the door for payback, she is setting herself up for more hurts. I will list the most prominent ones:

- ✓ She could become pregnant with another man's child while she is still married.

- ✓ She could become infected with STD. Some are curable, and some are not. Some could take her life, like Aids.

- ✓ The man she cheats with will have no respect for her, and he will not trust her. A relationship with him will likely end up in disaster too.

- ✓ The man who cheats with her is likely to cheat on her.

- ✓ Due to no-trust issues, she will inadvertently find herself moving from one relationship to the next.

- ✓ Several relationships over-time, in the end, usually leaves her with several children for different men, and she repeatedly finds herself stuck as a single mother.

- ✓ Usually, as she gets older, all of these failed relationships turns her into a hard woman, filled with bitterness and resentment. In the end, she realises that she might have hurt her cheating husband in a moment, but she had unwittingly hurt herself many times over, so it wasn't worth it. In the end!

Virtue Always Brings Victory

Because society has destroyed the man's psyche, the wise woman will not take revenge, but will win her husband's heart over, and over again by exhuming true (not false) virtue. She would command such levels of respect from him that he could change. His conscience will be so challenged that over-time he could learn to be faithful. **1 Peter 3:1** admonishes:

"Likewise, ye wives, be in subjection to your own husbands; that, if any obey not the word, they also may without the word be won by the conversation of the wives…"

Yes. A lot of men are dogs – whoremongers! But he has to find a woman with whom to become a dog. Therefore, if promiscuity is on the rise, it means then that many of the same women who are crying out against infidelity are guilty of the very same thing. As a result, it will be hard for the woman to convince the man that she would not return the favour and cheat on him, but if her virtue is real, after awhile, the truth will be evident. A genuinely virtuous woman who has also learned to be wise (not crafty) will eventually have her man eating out of her hand. His love and respect for her will also become evident.

Put On the Bond of Perfection

*H*aving now established each person's role in the marriage, for the union to continue in sweet harmony, the couple must put on the bond of perfection – love! What kind of love though?

The ancient Greeks have divulged that there are eight types of love:

"Eros" or Erotic Love. The first kind of love is Eros, which is named after the Greek god of love and fertility. ...

"Philia" or Affectionate Love. ...

"Storge" or Familiar Love. ...

"Ludus" or Playful Love. ...

"Mania" or Obsessive Love. ...

"Pragma" or Enduring Love. ...

"Philautia" or Self Love. ...

"Agape" or Selfless Love.

Naturally, husbands and wives will, at any point in their relationship, identify with all or most of these love experiences. However, the Agape or selfless love is the one that is of absolute value. Often a husband or wife will worry about whether or not the other loves them, but if they follow the principles of the Agape love, everything will fall nicely into place. That is, instead of worrying about being loved one should concentrate on loving, instead. Hence the principle in **Romans 14:13:**

"Let us not therefore judge one another any more: but judge this rather, that no man put a stumbling block or an occasion to fall in his brother`s way."

Therefore, if both persons equally apply this principle of giving love, rather than fretting about receiving love, then automatically, each person would be receiving love. Moses' law said 'do unto others as they have done to you." Jesus' law says *"And as ye would that men should do to you, do ye also to them likewise." – St. Luke 6:31 (KJV). The NIV Bible* says it this way: *"Do to others as you would have them do to you."*

Spiritually, it is illegal to demand what you are not willing to give. You have to be that which you want. Anything less is not love, but selfishness.

CONCLUSION

Grace Makes Provision For Restoration

*S*o yes, God hates divorce, because He does not like to see us in pain, and because He hates disharmony. But He, knowing that we are fallen man, living in a fallen world, knows that *'it is impossible for offences not to happen in life…' (St. Mark 18:7 and St. Luke 17:1).* As such, Him being the Master Planner, He has undoubtedly made provisions in Grace to forgive and restore even in a divorce and remarriage scenario. In further understanding our fragile nature, He acknowledges that all men cannot bear the same burden. Hence He said: *"If it be possible as much as lieth in you, live peaceably with all men." – Romans 12:18.*

God does not and would never endorse a divorce. However, God recognises that divorce is an offence within the kingdom that will happen. He knows that every man has a breaking point. Jesus only made the point on principle that if a divorce AND REMARRIAGE occurs while the first covenant was still intact, then a chain event of adultery would have been put in motion, but the exception to this rule would be if infidelity were the cause of the divorce. This is called "the exception clause" and wherever God gives an exception, in His Grace, He has made provision.

Also, if a divorce happens for any other reason than infidelity and either one remarries, in that moment of new consummation, adultery is committed because the act violates the spiritual bond. Afterwards God returns and blesses the new union, having respect for the fact that the new covenant which has now been made is answering to the natural realm, and confirming that a legal marriage had also taken place.

God has already blessed your Union. Stay in the blessing Plan, and His peace will rest upon you. Shalom!

Please stay on board to enjoy an exciting short story of four young Christian girls who found love, but who had their struggles as it relates to their approach to dating and courtship, balanced on the merit of their faith in Jesus Christ and their Church's doctrine.

Chapter 1 – **Four Friends Meet Up!**

*A*bigail Johnson maneuvered her blue 2008 330i BMW sedan into the parking lot of the Chicken Wings fast food restaurant. She was coming there to meet up with her three close friends, Sonya, Althea and Nadine. It was Friday evening, and a ritual for them to meet up at their favourite spot to recap on the week that was. She was like the unofficial leader of the quartet. They were all devout Christians, but Abigail had a warm, caring personality that easily drew people to her. She was totally surrendered to Jesus Christ. She genuinely loved people, and her three friends often looked to her for wise counsel.

As she got inside the restaurant and walked over to their favourite little corner where her friends were already seated, she noted that they were all just sitting there with silly, pleased looks on their faces. Just sitting there, waiting for her. She was late, which is not usual for her, but some extra work at the office had held her back. Her position as the assistant manager of the small city's second largest bank, The Dinero Commercial, kept her quite busy.

Despite that being their usual spot to meet up with each other on Fridays after work, this evening's meet up was spiked with an air of bated expectation and muted excitement. Althea had something very important to tell them, but she was not about to let the puss out of the bag until Abigail was present.

As Abigail slid into her seat, she took in their expressions. She could feel the aura of anticipation and could not help but wonder what kind of news Althea had, that had generated such an air of expectancy among the girls. Her eyes searched Althea's face for a clue, but apart from the fact that she was clearly holding back her excitement, her expression did not betray her secret.

Althea promptly beckoned for the waitress to come over and take their order. She declared that dinner was on her, which was not the norm. Usually, all of them would pool their money together, but this evening Althea decided to foot the Bill. They all looked at each other with pleased expressions. Whatever Althea had to tell them had to be epic.

Usually, they would hold hands, and pray before partaking of their meal. Then they would begin their girls' small talk while they ate. But this evening, before the "amen" was properly uttered, to end the prayer, Abigail gushed: "I have found him!"

Everyone looked at each other. Puzzled expressions now replaced the girlish excited looks that had been etched on their faces before. Althea was always a little dramatic, even about some simple things at times, so they all began to wonder, what is she coming with now, and to whom was she was referring.

"I have found my husband!"

Their expressions of bewilderment were gone, and excitement returned to their faces. They were all tuned in now. The four had been praying to the Lord for a husband. All three were dating, except for Althea. The plan was that they all would get married together. Their wedding day would shut down the city. It would be the talk of the town. But they had been waiting for Althea to get hitched to move forward with their plan.

They were all lovely young ladies. They were well educated, and all in good jobs. Althea was the Manager at a jewellery store, Sonya worked as a nurse at the local hospital, and Nadine was a High School Teacher. Abigail had just been promoted to Assistant Manager at the Dinero Commercial Bank.

"You found your husband?" Nadine yelled. "Is he someone that we know. What's his name?"

"OK. Kool it. Give her a chance to tell us." Sonya laughed. "Go ahead now, tell us. Who is this lucky guy?"

"Girl!" Abigail exclaimed, playfully pushing against Sonya. "You, also, need to give her a chance too, to tell us. Come on Althea, tell us already!" Then they all burst out laughing.

"We had met online. Facebook, to be specific…" Althea began.

"When. How long ago was this?" Nadine interrupted.

"Nadine…!" Abigail scolded jokingly. "Go on Althea, tell us everything. All the juicy details." They all laughed, drawing curious stares from some of the other patrons.

"Let's keep it down," Abigail whispered. "Go on now child. Tell us! Tell us!" She laughed.

Althea opened her phone and beckoned them to take a look. "This is him!" She exclaimed gleefully.

"Pepe Smith?!" The other three girls exclaimed in unison.

"Yes!" Althea beamed! They all knew Pepe Smith. His real name was Andre` Smith, but he was nicknamed Pepe after the Portuguese football star, for his hard-tackling defensive style on the football field. Pepe Smith had attended high school with them. He was very popular with the girls. Althea had always had a crush on him, but he never noticed her. So this came as a shock to all of them. Moreover, Pepe had moved away with his parents after high school.

"I didn't know Pepe was back in town. And you, and Pepe?!" Sonya remarked.

"No. He is not back in town. We hooked up on Facebook. He found me. And the best part is, he is now a Christian."

"Wow. That's awesome!" Abigail exclaimed. "But it's still a big surprise. A big whammo! Never would I have dreamt that you, and Pepe-!"

Althea looked hurt. "No, Thea. I didn't mean anything by it. It's just that, back in High School I knew you always liked him, but he was so busy with all the other girls, that he never had time for you. And now, out of the blues, all in one breath, it seems, you are telling us that you have found your husband and that he is Pepe Smith." Abigail explained. "But I am happy for you honey." She added.

'We all are!" The other girls chimed in.

They talked for the next hour or so, wherein Althea divulged how he had found her on Facebook. He was her senior in High School and had left town almost immediately after he had graduated. That was eight years ago. She was now twenty-four.

Pepe Smith was not just a Christian. He was a youth Pastor in his church. He was living two hours drive away from their city and had never married. They had been communicating by phone and social media, now, for almost three months. She did not say anything to her friends, because she wanted to make sure that this was real. Now he has decided to visit her that weekend. She was ecstatic.

The girls beamed at her. Abigail hugged her. "We are so happy for you, Thea. The Lord is just working things out for us."

Abigail herself was dating the youth Pastor at their church. Sonya and Nadine both were dating doctors.

"Two youth pastors, two doctors!" Sonya giggled.

"Yes. Isn't that something? We are paired up." Nadine laughed.

Abigail slipped into a reflective mood, while the girls chattered. She thought about how she and her fiancé, Wayne had met, and how their relationship had transpired to this point. They were now engaged to be married.

Chapter 2 – Abigail and Wayne

*T*here was a week-long crusade at their church. On the third night of the service, during Altar Call, she saw a tall young man made his way through the congregation, and up to the Altar. She was sitting in the Choir. That gave her a commanding view of all who were in attendance. He immediately caught her attention. He was light-skinned, with short, curly hair. She had never seen him before. It was a relatively large church. However, it was not so large that she would not have known if he had been in attendance at the meetings before. Especially for the fact that he had a commanding presence. He was not dashingly handsome, but there was something really attractive about him. And he was nicely dressed.

He simply came up to the Altar and knelt down, with his head bowed. After a while, she noticed that his shoulders had begun to shake uncontrollably. He was weeping. One of the Altar Ministers, a Deacon went over to minister to him. They were there for a while, even after everyone had dispersed, and the service had come to an end. That night Wayne Gallimore gave his life to the Lord, Jesus Christ.

He had just lost his mother to Cancer. She had died peacefully, her lips softly whispering the name of Jesus. At first, he was devastated by the way that Cancer had ravaged her body, but he was moved by her faith in Jesus, and how calmly she had transitioned from this life and into the next. There was a presence in the room as he watched her go. The love of God just filled up the place. Her pastor and a few brethren were there. Everyone was weeping softly. When he looked at them, to his amazement, their expressions were not of sorrow, but a strange glow seemed to emanate from them. He always thought that death was something to fear, but apparently, now, it wasn't. He was looking at the woman whom he loved so much – who had given birth to him, and who had nurtured him so well, embraced death as if it was the ushering of a new and better life. He had never truly believed in God before, even though his mother had always been a devout Christian. But that strange experience at his mom's passing melted his Atheistic resolve. He had suddenly begun to feel a hunger for this God in whom he had never believed.

He had heard about the meeting at church and decided to attend. His mother had been an ardent member for years. He wanted to visit the church that had taught his mother about God's amazing love. He wanted to have that peace. And he found it that night at Marvelous Love Ministries.

Wayne was eager for the word. Abigail watched him over the months that he had been converted, observing his eagerness to learn about God. However, she deliberately avoided him. She was developing feelings for this young convert but did not want to appear as if she was throwing herself at him. One Sunday after church he ambushed her.

As she beelined to the side door, he made a few quick steps, reaching her before she could make her exit.

"Sister Abigail, could you wait up for a minute, please."

She froze. Wayne Gallimore did not just call her name. She quickly gained her composure and turned to face him. "Certainly, brother Wayne. How may I help?"

"I don't mean to be forward, but I can't help but notice, that since I came to this church, it seems as if you have been avoiding me." He responded. He was not hesitant in his tone. She herself was a picture of loveliness, and guys are usually so awed by her that they would come across as bumbling fools. She smiled at the thought. But this Wayne Gilmore was anything but shy. He was not arrogant, just confident. That shook her up and made her nervous. She was not used to that level of male confidence matching her awesome presence.

"Whatever gave you that idea, brother?" She asked.

"Your very obvious avoidance." He returned.

"And why would I be avoiding you?" She countered.

"I can't seem to figure out why." He smiled. "It certainly cannot be because I pose a threat."

"I am sure that not everyone has spoken to you since you started attending this church, apart from usual greetings, which we all partake of.'

"You are quite right, but no one has been pointedly avoiding me. If I had done or said anything that offended you -."

"Oh! No! Whatever gave you that idea? We have barely spoken to each other. Only in greetings."

"Exactly. So I am curious as to why."

"Brother Wayne, I am not avoiding you. I have no reason to."

"I will not say that you are lying, but you are clearly not too good at hiding the truth." He smiled.

She flushed. He was right, but his smile softened the blow. She was a terrible liar. And she should be. After all, she was a Christian and should never lie, but how can she blurt out to this man that she was falling for him, and did not want her feelings to betray her?

That was the beginning of her love journey with Wayne St. Patrick Gallimore. Two years after conversion, and a few Bible courses, he was ordained as Youth Pastor. His dedication to God was phenomenal.

"Come back to us, Abby." Sonya laughingly jarred her out of her reverie.

Abigail looked at her friend and smiled. "Sonya. Sweet Sonya" She thought.

Chapter 3 – Sonya and Jarrett

Sonya had always loved nursing. As a little girl, she would set up her small hospital in the yard, using every living creature that she could lay her hands on, as patients. She had a few dollies that were permanent patients. They were always sick and needed her care.

After much sacrifice and prayers, her parents were able to send Sonya through nursing school. She finally got her Bachelor's Degree as a Registered Nurse.

At Tranquil Hospital, her experience with Dr Jarrett Duncan was volatile from the get-go. He was in charge of her ward. He was always short with her and would give her the hardest tasks. He would, from time to time, call her into his office to scold her about trivial things.

"I don't know what his problem is." Sonya would often cry to the girls. "I love my job, and I am always going way beyond the call of duty. But for him, I never seem to do anything right."

"Maybe he loves you, and doesn't know how to show it." Althea had teased.

"Cut it out." Said Abigail, coming to Sonya's defense. "Can't you see that the girl is devastated?"

"A fine way of showing his love, if that is what it is," Nadine commented. "If I were you, I would tell him a piece of my mind."

"Then he would get me fired." Sonya had wailed.

One day, as she was walking down the corridor, making her rounds, on turning a bend, she suddenly came face to face with Dr Duncan. She was startled but managed not to show it. "Dr Duncan." She greeted without breaking her stride. As she passed by him, he grabbed her hand, spun her round to face him, and kissed her flush on her mouth.

"Dr Dunc-!" She sputtered in shocked disbelief. He kissed her again. Then, as suddenly as he had grabbed her, he let go and went on his way.

"Nurse, see me in my office in five minutes!" He ordered, as he continued on his way.

Sonya had stood, rooted to the spot. She was confused, shocked and angry at the same time. She quickly looked around to see if anyone had seen what had just transpired. The hallway was empty. Thank God. But apparently, Dr Duncan had not cared about the cameras that had witnessed his rude, inappropriate behaviour.

"I should come to his office?" Sonya breathed angrily. "Who does this arrogant man think that he is? To the Administrator's office is where I should go to report this." But she had decided against it. She was still on probation and did not want to create waves around herself. She wanted an explanation and an apology, so she stormed into his office.

"Dr Duncan, I need an instant apology -!"

"Nurse Peters, I am sorry." Dr Duncan uttered. She was taken aback. Just as he had shocked her in the hallway with his strange behaviour, she was now equally amazed at his demeanour now. He had a look on his face that she had never seen before. He looked humble. She suddenly felt her head pounding. None of this was making any sense to her. She got kissed by a man who clearly loathed her, and now she was standing before the man, his visage was changed from the austere boss to a meek man, apologizing for his behaviour. But if all of that had shaken her up, his next words would rock her to the chore.

"Sonya, I love you!"

Sonya Peters felt the room sway under her feet. She could see the spotless floors rushing up to meet her face, then suddenly felt herself stop. The imminent impact froze in time. Sonya could feel his strong hands around her waist and realized that she had fainted. She was about to fall when he caught her, just in time. He held her for a moment until he was satisfied that she could stand upright on her own. Sonya hated to admit it to herself, but her protective embrace felt good. And she could smell the faint whiff of his cologne. It was nice.

"Are you OK?" He asked concern etched on his face.

She looked up into his face, too flustered to respond. "Y-yes!" She stuttered. "I demand an explanation!" Sonya said weakly, feeling annoyed with herself that her voice did not project the authoritative indignation that she had struck out for. He was a great kisser, and Sonya had involuntarily kissed him back. She felt annoyed with herself for having been so vulnerable. But then, she consoled herself that he had caught her off-guard.

Sonya's love journey with Dr Jarrett Duncan started right there. She was in love with him as well. Had been in love all this while. She just "hated him" too much to realize it at the time.

Jarrett Duncan was a Christian. He attended the Grace Baptist Church, two miles out of town. He had never married and had no children.

Chapter 4 – **Nadine and Curtis**

*N*adine Rose met Dr Curtis Samuels through Sonya and Jarrett. Dr Samuels, fresh from medical school had just joined Tranquility Hospital as an Intern.
Sonya liked working with Dr Samuels. He was witty, easy-going and also a Christian. She felt that Nadine, who was also easy-going, would like him. Besides, if he could forge a friendship with her, then she could show him around the city.

He was two inches shorter than Nadine. She did not like guys who were shorter than herself. She knew that Sonya was trying to hook her up, and she was eager, but she became skeptical when she stood in his presence and realized that she inched him by two.

The first chance she got during dinner that night, she dragged Sonya into the Ladies' Room.

"What were you thinking?" She started at Sonya as they entered the Rest Room. "You know how I hate it when men are shorter than I."

"I know honey, but relax. Get to know the guy. He is a darling."

"Yeah, maybe, but the height –"

"Nadine!"

"What?"

"Shut up! Height is not the only thing that makes up a person. Get to know the guy. Besides, you don't even know if he will like you like that. It's friends now, OK. Get to know him."

"OK." Sonya sighed resignedly.

Sonya was right. Before the night was out, Dr Curtis Samuels had them all in stitches! Nadine wanted to see him again and hoped that he would ask. He did, and she said yes. They were inseparable after that. Evidently, the good Doctor had grown some inches in her book. What he lacked in stature, he made up with his charming and humorous personality.

Chapter 5 – **Althea and Pepe**

*E*ventually, all three friends had been dating for a while, but no suitor was found for Althea. Well, the potential Suitors had found her, but she was never interested in anyone. She was always praying that she would see Pepe Smith again. She never stopped loving him. And, just like that, her prayers were answered, one evening, as she was home watching TV. She heard her Cell Phone ping. A Facebook message had come in. It was a friend request. She got those all the time from people whom she did not know and was about to delete it when the name caught her attention – Pepe Smith! She froze! Is this a joke. Pepe Smith?

She started scrolling through the pictures on his profile and could hardly contain her excitement. It was him! He now grew a small beard, but it was unmistakably him! She had often searched Facebook to try and locate him but to no avail. She had even tried using his correct name, but her efforts proved futile.

"Thank you, Jesus!" She squealed, punching the button to accept his friend request.

"What is it dear. Is something the matter?" Her mother asked from the adjoining room.

"No mother. It's OK." As close as she was with her mom, Althea was not about to share her find with anyone. At least, not yet. Then, suddenly, puzzlement replaced her excitement. Realization dawned on her that she was the one who had always loved Pepe, but he barely ever looked her way. She never really existed for him. He was too busy with his beautiful Belles to notice her. So why had he searched for her and sent her a friend request? Another ping came in. He was now messaging her. They exchanged numbers and chatted for hours.

As it turned out, he always liked her, but she was so pure, he did not want to taint her with his womanizing ways. He always secretly called her Cute Buttons. Two years after leaving school, one of his friends had died as a result of a drive-by shooting. He was sitting right next to his friend, but he was unscathed. The experience changed his life. He subsequently turned his life over to Jesus Christ. He now served in his church as the Youth Pastor.

She could not find him on Facebook before now because he was never on Facebook. But then, at the insistence of some of his young members, who called him "old diddy" for not having an account, he opened one. Then, on a hunch, he looked her up, and there she was, "bold and beautiful, as usual."

She flushed at the revelation that he had always liked her and referred to her as Cute Buttons, and smiled shyly against the phone in her ears. She was glad that he could not see her expression. She was surprised and pleased at the same time that he had always liked her, and that he had enough respect for her that he would want to protect her.

They had been dating online for a few months, and now he was coming to town that weekend to meet up with her. She was beside herself with excitement.

Chapter 6 – Girls Talk!

*E*verything was falling into place. God had answered their prayers. They had stayed faithful to Him, trusted Him, and now all of them had found love. All of them were heading towards the Aisles, and as they had wished, it was going to be a four-some wedding. Crazy! They girls brimmed with excitement.

Pepe had come that weekend. The reunion was awesome. Everybody had a good time. He started to visit more often, to stay close to Althea. She could not have been happier.

On another Friday evening, a few months after Althea's big announcement, the girls were snuggled up in Abigail's Living Room. They had decided not to go out that evening, and they were not going to meet up with their fiancés until the Saturday. This was girls' night in. Abigail had something on her mind that she wanted to talk about.

They held hands and prayed, then Abigail got right into what was on her mind.

"Girls, God had favoured us with our husbands. All fine men."

"Yes, He has." Althea beamed. Sonya and Nadine nodded in agreement.

"Which is why it is important that, as we honour Him in our daily living, we should also honour Him during dating and courtship." Abigail continued.

"I agree." Althea opined.

Nadine looked uncomfortable. "That is true, Abby, but what are you getting at. Is something wrong?"

"As you know, Wayne and I had been dating for about seven months now. Recently, the issue about sex before marriage came up between us –"

"Did you guys do it?" Nadine interrupted. A sly grin on her face.

"No, we did not do it," Abigail responded soberly. "There is an issue within church circles, wherein more and more people seem to believe that it is OK for an engaged couple to begin to have sexual intercourse before they get married." She continued.

"So what do you think about that Abby?" Althea asked. With veiled skepticism in her voice.

"Well, it is not just what I believe, but what the word of God says." Abigail declared. "Sex out of marriage is fornication, and fornication is a sin."

"B-but I have heard horror stories of folks getting married, without first having sex, and found out later that they were not compatible," Nadine stated.

"That might be true, but while sex is essential in a relationship, it must never be the foundation upon which the relationship is built. It must be built on other more enduring substance of the principles of God." Abby delivered. "There are other ways, other than breaking God's law, in which couples can find out if they are compatible before getting married."

"What other ways?" Althea asked.

"Pray to the Lord for direction. He said, acknowledge me in all your ways, meaning, our ways are the abilities that God has given us. However, even though God has endowed us with the ability to think and to act, He has not given us the inherent power to know the future. The reason for this partial impartation of power is that God wants us to be agents of free choice, but in the same breath, He does not want us to act independently of Himself. He wants us to partner with him for our own benefit, which is to His glory."

"Wow! Abby!" Sonya exclaimed. That is so true.

"After honouring God with our prayers, we can begin to use our abilities of communication. Be honest with your fiancé, and encourage him to be honest about anything that could adversely affect the relationship or about any concerns that both of you might have." Abigail continued. "And go to the doctor for a check-up before marriage."

Sonya was nodding in agreement. "Mm!" She sounded, reflectively.

Althea's discomfort had returned, and it was more evident this time.

"Althea are you OK?" Sonya asked concern showing on her face.

"Pepe and I are having sex!" She blurted out before Abigail could stop her.

"Althea, you did not have to divulge that here and now." She said, placing a hand on Althea's hand.

"I disagree, Abby," Sonya said. "We are all friends. We love and care about each other. What have we not told each other? What have we not discussed? This time should be no different. Tell us, Althea."

She and Pepe had been dating for four months now. They started having sex in the third month. It was Pepe who had raised the issue about sex. For the concern about incompatibility that Abigail had stated, he wanted to be sure that we were right for each other. He had told her that 'because they were engaged to be married, it would be ok to do it, as long as they stayed faithful to each other.'

Althea was a bit hesitant at first, but afterwards, she gave in because, secretly, she had always felt that she would never marry a man without first having sex with him.

Abigail looked at her with concern in her eyes. "Althea, there are some factors that you must consider. By engaging in sexual intercourse before marriage, the man could still marry you, but after the romantic ardour has cooled, he might begin to look at you narrowly, not trust you, and begin to lose respect for you. Or, two, after having tasted the goods, he could simply change his mind and not marry you."

"Pepe would never do that. We love each other." Althea said, looking down at her hands.

"Abby is right Althea," Sonya stated, reiterating her support for Abigail's line of talk.

"To each his own, I think." Nadine offered, shrugging her shoulders.

"Are you and Curtis having sex as well?" Sonya asked.

"To each his own, is all I'm saying," Nadine responded, avoiding the question. "So is Wayne in agreement with your take on the matter Abby. Doesn't he want to do it?"

"Wayne and I are in complete agreement on the matter, and we are committed to proceeding with our courtship, following the principles that I had mentioned."

"Oh!" Nadine uttered.

They spoke some more on the issue. In the end, Sonya was apparently in agreement with Abby, that, just as they had trusted God to send them right men, they should also believe God during dating and courtship, and do the right thing.'

Althea had something to think about, while Nadine was inconclusive regarding her take on the matter, merely stating that 'she would not judge anyone if they did it or not.'

Chapter 7 - All Aboard – Wedding Bells Ring!

*T*he day had finally arrived. The whole town was talking about it. The four best friends were all getting married in one big, flamboyant affair. It certainly had the hallmarks that it would be a memorable event. Family and friends from all over. Pepe's and Curtis' parents, and their church folks had come across. Excitement filled the air. Everyone was happy. The children were all running around gleefully. Everything could not have been more perfect. The four friends were merely beaming with happiness.

The four of them had agreed to stick with the tradition of making the grooms sweat a little, but not for more than an hour. They giggled at the thought.

The Ceremony was to be held at the Anglican Church, because of it's impressive stone walls and beautiful high, stained glass windows.

The evening was cool. Not humid as it usually is at this time of year. It was Summer. The beginning of that season. Perhaps, to honour the bride four, Summer had paused its stride and asked Spring to return for that moment to lend a whiff of its aura, to make this event one without heat and fluster.

The family and guests had arrived on time. They filed orderly, with hushed, excited chatter inside the sanctuary. The grooms would arrive soon, followed by the beautiful brides.

The event was plastered with colour, to the taste of the four brides: Lavender, Rose Pink, Blue and Gold Yellow.

The reception would be a garden affair, complete with flowers and colourful arrangements to match the mood and the choice of colours.

Abigail glanced over at the other girls, as the final touches to her make-up were being applied. They looked radiant. She still felt disappointed in Althea for having begun to have sex with Pepe before marriage. And Nadine –! She had acted bizarre last month when they had that meeting at her house. It felt as if she was guilty of something. Maybe she was sexually involved with Curtis as well. No! Abigail pushed the thought aside. She did not want to be guilty of judging. As she emerged from her thoughts, she caught Sonya looking at her, smiling.

"Where were you off to, now?" She queried.

"Nowhere. Was only thinking. Are you happy?" Abigail responded.

"Happy? I am over the Moon!" Sonya squealed.

"But it's not night as yet dear," Althea said with a happy, short laugh.

"An eclipse for her, maybe?" Nadine joined in. Everyone laughed!

"I am so happy for you girls." Abigail declared, her eyes aglow with love for her friends.

"And we are happy for you!" The girls chorused, as if they had practiced the part.

They were on schedule. The brides' limousines rolled up to the Church like royals. The girls had delegated Abigail's Limo to be up front. Sonya's, Nadine's and Althea's Limo followed in that order.

Abigail looked out and saw an Usher approach her vehicle. The driver rolled down the glass. "Ready?" He asked the Usher.

"Not quite. One of the grooms has not shown up as yet." He replied.

Abby overheard. "Maybe he is running a little bit late." She said, hoping that it wasn't Wayne. "Which groom is it?" She asked.

The Usher looked at the program. "Mr Curtis Samuels." He responded.

"Did anyone call to find out what held him up?" Abby queried.

"Someone was ringing his phone, but got no answer." The Usher revealed.

"Ok. Well, please go to each of the cars behind me, and inform the girls that Mr Samuels is running a bit late and that I am suggesting we drive around the block in the meantime. He should be here by the time we get back." Abigail said.

"Ok, ma'am. Will do." The Usher responded, moving along to deliver the news.

On receiving the news, Nadine felt disappointed. They all had agreed to be early, except for the Brides, who would be an hour late. Now, why is Curtis late? And why wasn't he answering his calls?

They drove around for another, fifteen minutes, then returned to the Church. Curtis had still not arrived, and he could not be reached on his cell phone. Everyone in the church was now getting restive, with puzzled looks on their faces. What was happening? What was holding up the wedding?

The girls became worried. Nadine had apprehension written all over her face.

After about an hour, while they still sat in the Limousines, they saw Curtis' family and church folks filing out of the Church, their heads held down.

"What is happening?" Nadine wailed, unable to keep her composure any longer.

The Usher came out from inside the church and went over to Abby's car.

"What is happening?" She echoed Nadine's frantic cry as if she had heard her from inside her own vehicle.

The Usher looked apologetic. "Mr Samuels called his mother and told her that he could not go through with the wedding. He is on a flight to Miami as we speak."

"Jesus!" Abigail whispered harshly under her breath. "Oh! God! Let me go and tell her." She told the Usher.

Nadine was beside herself. She was distraught! How could Curtis do this to her? He said that 'he loved her and would never hurt her.' He had given no indication of a change of heart. Up until last night, they had stolen away and made love to each other. He had loved her with such urgency – such passion! Her head began to spin. She could hear Abby's voice as if from a distance, echoing a command for someone to get a glass of water.

The next thing she knew was that she was lying in a bed at Tranquility Hospital. She had fainted, and they had rushed her over. The doctor declared that she was OK, but that he would hold her for another hour or so for observation. But Nadine was anything but OK. She was crushed. She felt used. Manipulated. She felt as if she was murdered. She wanted to die! The pain! The shame! Curtis Samuels had run out on her – on her wedding day! My God!

Abigail's words at their meeting came floating back to her:

"By engaging in sexual intercourse before marriage, the man could still marry you, but after the romantic ardour has cooled, he might begin to look at you narrowly, not trust you, and begin to lose respect for you. Or two, after having tasted the goods, he could simply change his mind and not marry you."

It was as if Abigail had known – as if she had seen the future. She never did admit to her friends that she and Curtis had started to have sex. Like Althea and Pepe, she and Curtis held the same belief that they had to test each other before marriage. After that, they began to have sex on a regular basis. She told herself that, even though it was a sin, God would understand and forgive them. Besides, they were getting married. But now she realized how wrong she was, and how very right Abigail was. She doubled up in the hospital bed and cried uncontrollably!

*T*he wedding had gone on as planned for the other three girls. It was now six months since that bitter-sweet day.

Immediately after their wedding, they had ushered Nadine off to the Bahamas for a two-week hiatus to get her head together. Unknown to her at first, the couples themselves had also honeymooned in the Bahamas, where they could keep a secret eye on her before adjoining their company to hers. They wanted to wait until she was much calmer, then come to her a couple of days before they flew back home and to work. Honeymoon was a week, but Nadine was booked for an extra week. She needed that time to recuperate and get her emotions level again.

Nadine was surprised to see them. She did not know that they were in the Bahamas because they had initially planned to honeymoon at a posh resort a few hours ride from their city. The girls had changed plans at the last minute for her sake. She flushed with gratitude for their consideration and embarrassment at what had happened.

As it turned out, Dr Curtis Samuels struggled with the fact that 'she had allowed herself to sleep with him, knowing that it was against the principles of Christ. He admitted that he was guilty of sinning as well, but he felt that she should have held her integrity intact.'

"What a low-down hypocrite!" Sonya breathed angrily.

"My thoughts exactly!" Abigail said in agreement.

Althea was noticeably silent. Then no one spoke.

"That could have easily happened to me as well." She said, breaking the awkward silence.

Still, no one said a word. The moment was too embarrassing. Abigail placed a hand on her shoulder.

"Well, in spite of me, all is well that ends well." Nadine offered with a strained smile. But little did they know that their troubles were far from over.

Chapter 8 – Stormy Clouds On The Horizon!

The first sign of any one of the girls' marriages unravelling was Sonya and Jarrett.

They all had embarked on their new lives, with their loves. Everything was going great. They were all happily married. It was now almost two years since their nuptials. Nadine had gotten over Curtis and was dating someone from where she worked at the High School. She had vowed to keep her dating and courtship clean this time. She now fully embraced the principles that God had laid down for a healthy relationship. It was terrific to see her bubbly again.

Their little girls' meetings were not as frequent as before, because of family responsibilities. They would meet like two Fridays in a given month.

This evening was one of those Fridays that they got to meet. Sonya came in a worried look on her face. She wasted no time. She just got into it.

"Jarrett is divorcing me!" As the words gushed from her mouth, the tears rushed to her eyes.

"What?!" Everyone uttered at once in disbelief!

"Divorce?" Abigail shouted, grabbing her by the arm. Before now, there was never any indication that Sonya's marriage was in problems. Tearfully, she laid it out for them.

"Abby." She said. "At that meeting in your Living Room, you mentioned the dangers of sex before marriage. But we missed out something."

"What was that?" Abby asked. Puzzled.

"I was in full agreement with you, and I never slept with Jarrett before we got married. We kept our dating and courtship clean."

"So, what happened then?" Althea asked impatiently.

"The part that we missed was that God had given consent to Jarret and me because we had built our relationship with Christ and His principles. But after we got married, we never continued to build our marriage on those same principles. I was not the submissive wife as I should have been. And he, in turn, did not exert himself as the head of the household, according to Christ's instructions. I began to disdain him for not holding up his end, and he, in turn, got turned off my rebellious streak. We both did a good job in keeping this under-wrap until he started seeing one young nurse at the hospital."

"Jesus! Sonya, stop it. Don't say that!" Althea shouted!"

"It's true." Sonya sighed. He told me that she was humbler than I. And that he was sorry, but he did not love me anymore." She sobbed. She opened her purse and took out some papers. These are the papers.

A month later, their divorce was final. Sonya eventually moved away, to work at another hospital in a neighbouring city. It was too much for her to work in the same hospital with Jarrett and his new woman. The last she heard was that they were getting married.

One day at work, Abigail's line rang. It was her secretary. "Mrs Gallimore, there is a Mrs Althea Smith here to see you." She said.

"Oh. Yes. Send her in please."

It was not unpleasant, but it was unusual for anyone of her friends to visit her at work. It must be important, or urgent. She hoped that everything was alright.

"Hi, Thea. This is a wonderful surprise!" She exclaimed. Coming around her desk to hug Althea as she came into the office. There was trouble, she could see it in Althea's eyes. "What's wrong? Have a seat."

Althea broke down before she could properly seat herself.

"I am going to divorce Pepe!"

"Oh. No! Not again!" Abigail groaned. "Thea. What now?"

It was now two years and three months since they had gotten married. Sonya became a divorcee one month shy of her two-year marriage, and now Althea! It was just too much.

Her indiscretion with Pepe during their courtship had come back to haunt them. Abigail's words echoed like prophecy. Pepe had indeed married her. The sex was great. But a few months ago, his behaviour towards her had begun to change. He did not pay as much attention to her as he once did. He would often speak to her in disrespectful tones, and he had begun to search her phone. If she came home from work a little later than he thought she should, he would get upset and asked what took her so long. He suddenly did not trust her. She never gave him any reason to doubt her loyalty.

She hid all this well from her friends, but this morning he slapped her.

"W-whaat??!!" Abby could not believe what she was hearing. It was then that Abigail noticed the bruise under her eye. It was hidden under make up and her hair. But on closer scrutiny, it could be seen.

"It's not the first time he hit me." Althea divulged.

"My God! Abigail placed her hand over her mouth.

"This is the fourth time, and I have had enough."

Their divorce became final within a couple of months.

God indeed had forgiven Althea for her sinning against him during courtship, just like He had forgiven Nadine and Sonya for not continuing to build her marriage the same way that she had been mindful during her courtship, but the consequences were still there to bear.

Chapter 9 – Mr and Mrs Wayne Gallimore

*I*t has been twelve years since Abigail and Wayne got married. They now have two lovely children, one girl and a boy. Wayne was currently the Senior Pastor at their Church.

Abigail could not have asked for a better husband, father and Pastor. They were merely best friends and lovers.

Abigail Johnson had surrendered her will the Jesus Christ. During her dating and courtship with Wayne, they both fully embraced the principles that God had laid down for successful dating and courtship. Afterwards, during marriage, they both submitted to their roles as God had ordained it.

Wayne Gallimore led his household by example. He was the priest of the home. He did everything he could to enhance his family. He was awesome.

Abigail understood that for the harmony of her home to prevail she had to come in agreement with her husband humbly. Their children were inspired by the partnership between their mom and dad.

Nobody in that household was perfect, by far, but they all stayed honest and sincere at the feet of Jesus. And everything stayed in its proper order. Harmony prevailed. Prosperity reigned. The Gallimores never experienced divorce.

The Mathematics of Tithing and Offering

is now available on Amazon.

Courtesy of

Please note: The preceding story spoke of true life circumstances within the Body of Christ. However, all the characters portrayed were created by the writer and bears no reference to anyone in real-life.

"...Jesus answered and said, I thank You, O Father, Lord of heaven and earth, because You have hid these things from the wise and prudent, and have revealed them to babes."

(St. Matthew 11:25 - AKJV)

For more information visit us on Facebook

@MarvelousLoveMinistries

Our Website: marvelousloveministries.com is coming soon.

For speaking engagements you may e-mail me at: marvelousloveministries@gmail.com

or call me at : 1(345) 323-2770

www.ingramcontent.com/pod-product-compliance
Lightning Source LLC
Chambersburg PA
CBHW042331150426
43194CB00001B/17